MARGARETHA MONTAGU

Mindfulness and Meditation Options

This book was professionally typeset on Reedsy.
Find out more at reedsy.com

FEATURING EQUINE-GUIDED MINDFULNESS MEDITATION

MARGARETHA MONTAGU

MINDFULNESS AND MEDITATION OPTIONS

A COMPREHENSIVE GUIDE TO SUCCESSFUL STRESS MANAGEMENT

Contents

Front Page

Mindfulness and Meditation Options

Featuring Equine-guided Mindfulness Meditation
Staying focused in a fast-paced World

By Dr Margaretha de Klerk
(nom de plume: Margaretha Montagu)
MargarethaMontagu.com
EquineGuidedGrowth.com
MargarethaMontagu@gmail.com

Invitation

Would you like to escape on a virtual visit to the sun-blessed south of France?

Of course you do!

Join me on a virtual visit to one of the most unspoilt parts of south-west France, where you can meet our horses and lose yourself in the gorgeous pictures of the meadows, mountains, lakes, orchards, vineyards, lost-in-time villages, decadently delicious food and outstanding wines of this region while you listen to some of the most beautiful French chansons ever written.

All you have to do is to fill in your e-mail address below and subscribe to my blog where you will find empowering tips, motivating quotes, inspiring articles and lots of how-to blog posts. Subscribers receive a copy of my 10 Steps to Instant Self-Confidence guide - straight from the horse's mouth!

Reading my blog will enable you to
  Discover what is wrong with the south of France
  Read more about mindfulness meditation and find your own way to a better practice
  Use mindfulness and meditation to free yourself from your immobilising fear and deal with stress more effectively
  Get access to my equine-guided mindfulness meditation online

course

Find out more about equine-assisted personal development and how to connect with horses

and learn how to make a decadently-delicious Mousse au Chocolat Noir.

Go to my website at EquineGuidedGrowth.com and fill in your e-mail address to receive news of my workshops here in the south of France with details of last-minute discounts and early bird special offers, available only to my mailing list subscribers. Your adventure starts right away and you will shortly be off to the south of France! Your e-mail address is 100% safe and you can unsubscribe from my blog at any time.

Dedication

I dedicate this book to my horses. To Aurileo d'Alegria and to Beau de la Babinière, who have left this world for a better one but who I still miss with all my heart nearly every day, to Belle de la Babinière, my soul mare, to Tess des Sources Sacrées, to the Duc D'Alegria, to Aurore d'Alegria and to Bass des Sources Sacrées, my current and constant companions and to Senador du Domaine de Passage, a soul mate from another stable, thank you for everything you have taught me so far and are still teaching me every day. My life has changed beyond all recognition since you came to live with us, enriched a thousand-fold.

About the Author

About the Author

Dr Margaretha Montagu (MBChB, MRCGP, NLP cert, Counselling cert, Med Hyp Dip and EAGALA cert level 2)

Qualifications, Interests and Experience

You only really need to read this chapter if you wonder what qualifications and experience I have that would make this book a worthwhile read. Right, so I am a medical doctor. I worked as a doctor, mostly with women, for 20+ years. I retired early, partly because of a debilitation eye condition and partly because I became frustrated with the limitations of my profession. I always wanted to own a horse or two, so when I could no longer work as a doctor, I bought Belle de la Babinière, a stunningly handsome Friesian mare and well aware of it. I discovered that horses are like crisps, you can never have only one. I bought Beau de la Babinière, a drop-dead-gorgeous Lusitano stallion. I retrained in equine-assisted experiential learning. I now host Connect with Horses personal empowerment workshops to help women and the odd man to be more confident, to cope better with stress and to communicate more effectively.

As a medical doctor, I have always been interested in stress management. Over the years, I worked in a variety of specialities, including psychiatry, and I came to the conclusion that many diseases have their roots in my patients' inability to handle stress. Instead of treating stress-related and stress-induced illnesses, I decided I would prefer to help my patients prevent stress from causing or worsening disease and ruining their health.

Writings

Somewhere along the line, I started writing. I discovered that being grateful for one's blessings is a great stress management tool. I started writing a gratitude diary. I enjoyed writing so much that I started a blog. I intended the blog to be a shop window showcasing our region, our horses, and our workshops. It quickly became much more. Browsing my blog is indeed a bit like visiting us virtually, but it is also a library filled with articles about confidence building, problem-solving, strengthening relationships, conflict resolving and much more. Eventually, I gathered some of my best blog posts into a book.

My book is called Self-Confidence made Simple: 16 Frenchwomen share their Self-esteem Secrets (you can read a preview of this book in the last chapter.) I wrote a second book called You ARE Good Enough! Secure Your promising, purposeful and prosperous Future came next. I also wrote a book for horse riders who have lost their horse riding confidence: Horse Riding Confidence Secrets. I am currently working on my next book. Subscribers to my blog's mailing list will be notified when it is published. During the launch, my mailing list subscribers can usually download a preview of my new book for free, for a limited time. Before I publish the book, I send a free copy to each of the members of my VIP Readers Group for review. If you would like to join this group, please send an e-mail to margarethamontagu@gmail.com with "VIP Readers" as the subject.

On-line Presence

When I researched this book, I collected a huge number of quotes, articles and blog posts. I share these on Pinterest at Margaretha' Muse and on Twitter @EquineGuidedMD. I am on Goodreads and on LinkedIn as Margaretha Montagu, but the best place to find out more about my books is my Margaretha de Klerk Amazon Author page. I have a Facebook page that I use as an aide-memoire: Margaretha Montagu's Workshops and Books.

There is something I want you to know.

Despite all my experience, knowledge and qualifications, I am no different from you. I am far from perfect. I do not always practice what I preach. I do not have the answers to all my questions and I do not have the solutions to all my problems. Like you, I sometimes feel confused and overwhelmed. I am, however, convinced that mindfulness meditation - especially with horses - can make a huge difference to your life. My hope is that the content of this book will help you as much as it helped me.

Foreword

Dear Reader

Thank you so much for buying this book, I am sure that you are going to benefit enormously from reading it. To explain why I am so sure, I need you to understand WHY I wrote this book, my longest book to date. There must be hundreds of books and e-books on the market about mindfulness and thousands about meditation. If you are interested in meditation, you have probably read several excellent books already.

So why did I write yet another book about mindfulness and meditation? It wrote this book because I want to share with you how absolutely awesome equine-guided mindfulness meditation is. Take it from me, there is nothing else quite like it. Even if you are not that keen to come face to face with a horse (because they are HUGE and might be dangerous and even deadly,) you will find this book valuable way beyond your expectations.

I only recently discovered how powerful equine-led mindfulness meditation can be. I hosted Connect with Horses personal empowerment workshops here in the south of France, based on equine-assisted personal development for the past 10 years. I have long known what a tremendous difference it can make to my clients' lives. In the last three years, I added equine-guided meditation to the mixture, so meditating in the presence of horses is not entirely new to me. In the equine-guided meditation chapter in this book, you can read about how I "accidentally" discovered this practice. It was only in the last 18 months though, that I discovered how much it could help me, personally.

In the last 18 months, due to my ongoing eye problems, I have not been able to ride much. I am seriously into classical riding, or dressage, as it is also known. I have been obsessed with studying this riding discipline for the last ten years. Not being able to ride regularly, as I had to have one eye operation after another, was mind-numbing. I had to find something else to do with my horses. I had to find a different way to be with my horses. I fell deeper into equine-guided meditation, once again, more or less by accident, rather than by design. My eye surgeon advised me not to do anything that could precipitate another retinal detachment. As far as I could gather, that meant that all I could do with the horses was be with them, without actually doing anything.

If you know me, you will understand how crippling not being able to do anything is to me.

I already knew that just being in the presence of horses can be an exercise in mindfulness meditation. Now I discovered that watching them graze through the window on the days that I could not go outside could work as well as a mindfulness meditation exercise. I discovered that in the long and often painful hours of the night, that looking at pictures of my horses is as effective as seeing them in real life. Same goes for looking at video of horses grazing peacefully. My ultimate discovery was that I could mindfully meditate, just by imagining being with my horses. I have read, when I studied visualisation, that our minds cannot distinguish between what we imagine is happening and what is really happening. You can read more about this method of meditation in the "Visualisation Meditation" chapter of this book.

While in hospital, I tried imagining that I am actually with the horses, making it as real as I possibly could by using all five my senses (down to the aroma and taste of the first cup of coffee of the morning that I usually have while I watch them through the kitchen window.) I found that this sort of visualisation meditation is as powerful - maybe even more so! - than had I been within touching distance of my horses. If you have read some of my other books you may know that I highly recommend journaling, even if you start small by keeping a bullet-point gratitude diary. As is my custom, I kept a diary of my experiences and in this latest edition of this book, I share with you what I have learned: about myself, about mindfulness meditation and about the mind-blowing soothing and healing ability of horses.

As I got better, I added some of my other favourite meditation methods to the equine-guided model. Walking meditation became mindfully walking and meditating with horses. Working meditation became grooming horses mindfully while meditating. Music meditation became listening to music with the horses and noting the effect it has on them, especially drumming. Writing meditation became making an equine-inspired gratitude list. Etc.

This book, which I wrote originally as an accompanying workbook to our workshops, is now about sharing my discoveries with not only our workshop participants but with everyone who has ever felt drawn to horses and is interested in mindful meditation. When you have read this book, you will not only know a lot more about mindfulness but also a good deal about 12 different meditation methods, including equine-guided mindfulness meditation.

It is my dearest wish that this book will make a difference in your life, for the better and in the long-term. The ultimate intent of this book is not only to introduce you to equine-guided mindfulness meditation, but also equip you with a toolbox full of tools that will help cope with life's challenges as well as enable you to live a life full of purpose and meaning.

Btw, all the downloads mentioned in the e-book version of this book are free and that the book contains NO affiliate links. Also, I would also hugely appreciate it if you would let me know if you find spelling mistakes in the text. English is not my first language, so despite my best intentions, mistakes do slip in.

All the best,
  Margaretha

PS. Have you subscribed to my blog's mailing list yet? If you have already subscribed, thank you so much! If not, please do. It will enable me to continue to support you in your quest to become your best self, once you have finished reading this book. The aim of my blog is to assist you to make the most of yourself and to provide you with the tools to do so. The blog has a distinctly French flavour, as I also share with you our life here in the south of France. You can subscribe at my website and you will receive my 10 Steps to Instant Self-Confidence guide - straight from the horse's mouth!

Introduction

Have you ever wondered: (I know I have!)

Why do I attract so many challenging situations?

Why do I feel so tired all the time and why do I have no energy to accomplish anything?

This book can help you to re-condition your mind using mindfulness and meditation to stop attracting challenging events, situations and relationships into your life and instead attract success, energy, prosperity and abundance into your life. In this book, I introduce you to the tools I use during my personal empowerment workshops: equine-assisted experiential learning and a variety of mindfulness meditation methods, including equine-guided mindfulness meditation.

About this Book

Mindfulness and Meditation Options is the second book in the Fabriqué en France Series.
Also in this series:
- Self-Confidence made Simple: 16 Frenchwomen share their Self-esteem Secrets
- Embracing Change - in 10 minutes a Day
- You ARE good enough - 10 Simple Steps to Stop Sabotaging Yourself

Why read a book about mindfulness? Because mindfulness

- enables you to deal with distractions more effectively so that you can concentrate easily and increase your productivity both at home and at work
- makes you more creative and so that you can solve problems faster as it helps you to let go of doubts that might otherwise block your creativity
- helps you to sleep better at night so that you are not tired all the time and can get a lot more done during the day.
- enhances your mental agility and alertness, increases cognitive recall and protects you from memory loss as you get older
- gives you time to think before you act, making it easier to control your anger and listen more effectively so that you get on better with family, friends and colleagues
- dramatically lowers your stress levels so that you can cope effectively with the challenges that come your way. It also makes you physically and mentally healthier and more resilient while helping you avoid the damage stress can do to our minds and bodies
- makes you more compassionate towards others and towards yourself so that you can accept yourself, forgive yourself and love yourself just as you are

As with my book Self-Confidence Made Simple, I have also made a playlist for this book. It is called Equine Enchantment and you can watch it or listen to it on my YouTube channel (Margaretha Montagu), while you continue reading. The first video is about Andrea Bocelli, the blind opera singer. In the video, Andrea rides a beautiful dressage stallion, Sir César. For me, already blind in one eye and with ongoing problems in the other, this video has been immensely inspiring. Apart from having its own playlist, Mindfulness and Meditation Options differs from other books about mindfulness and meditation in five unique ways:

1. This book is not just a collection of explanations and instructions. It

is a book full of suggestions and solutions. I wrote this book because I passionately believe in the transformational power of mindfulness meditation, especially guided by horses. I believe that mindfulness and meditation are highly effective stress management strategies that can help practitioners avoid the physical and mental damage that stress can cause. That is why it is of primordial importance to me to help you find a meditation method that suits you, whether it is equine-guided on not. A method that you will be able to incorporate into your daily life without having to sacrifice too much of your precious time. A method that you will be able to continue practising daily, for the rest of your life.

2. This book proposes a technique, in the form of a questionnaire, to help you choose the meditation method will work the best for you. Meditation is not a one-size-fits-all exercise. We are all different, we each have to find a meditation method that suits us, mentally and physically.

3. This book helps readers solve real-life problems. In each chapter, an everyday person with everyday challenges explains his/her problem. There is

- someone who struggles to lose weight and keep it off,
- someone with relationship problems,
- someone who cannot sleep,
- someone with an overwhelmingly stressful job,
- someone whose new business is faltering,
- someone who is trying to make a long-treasured dream come true,
- someone who wants to grow spiritually...

The rest of each chapter demonstrates how each of these people can solve their problem with mindfulness and meditation.

4. This book contains a chapter explaining what equine-guided mind-

fulness meditation is and how to practise it.

5.   This book (the e-book version) is an interactive and practical aid – each chapter contains a selection of links to further resources, carefully chosen to help the reader discover and experience the various meditation methods presented. There are also links to scientific studies that back up the effectiveness of the methods described in the book.

Mindfulness and Meditation Options aims answer your questions about mindfulness and meditation and especially about equine-guided mindfulness meditation. In this book, I also investigate the scientific studies that have been conducted about both mindfulness and meditation. I will introduce you to a variety of different meditation methods:
    walking meditation,
    working meditation,
    writing meditation,
    music meditation,
    visualisation meditation,
    contemplative meditation,
    equine-guided meditation and gratitude meditation
    sleep meditation
    as well as breathing meditation.

Each chapter starts with a letter written to me by a potential participant in one of the personal empowerment workshops we host here in the south of France. Each letter reveals a specific problem, or set of problems that readers will be able to identify with. The letter is followed by a detailed explanation of how to solve the writer's problems using mindfulness and meditation. If you too would like to find out more about mindfulness and meditation and how it can benefit you in a practical and sustainable way, this is the book for you.

This book will introduce you to the tools, mindfulness and meditation, with or without horses, that you need to completely transform your life into exactly what you want it to be.

Preparation

Not all meditation methods are equal. There are many different meditation methods and although they all have the same objective, creating inner peace, they use different techniques to achieve a common set of goals. Some meditation methods are more effective at promoting relaxation while other forms have a greater impact on relieving depression or on counteracting the impact of trauma. Others improve your focus or enhance your ability to be compassionate and kind.

Because everyone has a different mental make-up, the best type of meditation for each one of us is a highly individual choice. What works for someone else will not necessarily work for you. Usually, you have to try several different methods to see which one suits you best.

To find out which practice is best for you, ask yourself these questions:

1) What specific benefits are you looking for? Are you looking for a stress-reducing tool? Would you like to be able to concentrate better? Do you need help with anger management? Are you looking for a cure for insomnia? Do you have health problems? We all have our own reasons for researching and trying mindfulness and meditation.

2) Which meditation method is of interest to you? Are you interested in mindfulness meditation, loving-kindness meditation, visualisation meditation, insight meditation or even equine-guided meditation?

3) How much time can you allocate to meditation and how often do you intend to practise meditation? Some people only meditate while on retreat, others meditate daily. Some meditate for an hour or more a day, others can only meditate for ten minutes at a time and not always every day.

4) Is this your first time or have you meditated before? If yes, which

method did you use? Did it work for you? If not, why not?

5) Do you want to stick to one meditation method or do you are you open to trying a combination of different methods?

6) How soon would you like to start experiencing benefits? Meditating for longer and more often will give you access to a wider range of benefits.

7) Is this a long-term commitment or a short-term problem-solving intervention? For example, do you need to find a way to relax because you find yourself in a temporarily stress-inducing situation or do you want to manage a long-term pain-producing illness?

Make a note of your replies to these questions, we are going to come back to them later. The reason I recommend that you ask yourself these questions is to help you clarify your expectations. It is important to remember, as you make decisions about meditation methods, that whatever method you choose, for however frequently or for however long you choose to meditate, you don't have to be a long-term meditation expert to benefit.

While researching their book, Altered Traits: Science Reveals How Meditation Changes Your Mind, Body, and Brain, Richie Davidson and Daniel Goleman looked at the results from the very best scientific studies - 6,000 studies have been published so far and mindfulness was the single most-studied method. They wanted to find evidence that meditation creates long-term, lasting effects rather than only short-term effects that vanish once you stop your meditating. They discovered that the data shows a powerful impact from meditation right from the beginning. The more hours you meditate, the more benefits you enjoy.

In Chapter 3, I will introduce you to a very effective technique that will help you determine which meditation method, or combination of meditation methods, is best for you.

Chapter 1

What is Meditation?

"The soul always knows what to do to heal itself. The challenge is to silence the mind."
  Caroline Myss

Meditate, moi? I didn't think so.

I used to be sceptic about meditation. I had a vague notion of what meditation is and that people meditate to relax. Being as obsessed with stress management as I am, that did sound marginally interesting. It is just that sitting still for hours on end did not appeal to me at all. Honestly, I had way too much to do to waste time sitting around doing nothing the whole day long. There aren't enough hours in the day as it is.

I did notice, as I suspect all horse owners and many horse riders do, that when I spend time with my horses, just being with them, I tend to end up in a more peaceful place spiritually. I also discovered that when I am with one or more of my horses, being mindful is easier, nearly effortless. I benefit physically and mentally, on a cold winter's morning, from taking my soul mare Belle into the barn and grooming her unhurriedly, gently easing away the knots in her muscles and basking in her unconditional love and quiet understanding, far from the worries and troubles of my average day.

It was only, when a meditating friend said to me, "You know, you already meditate, without even realising, for long periods every day, when you are with your horses. I have seen you at it many times," that I sat up and took notice. Meditate, moi?

I didn't think so.

"Oh yes," she said, "when you are grooming the horses, you become so focused on what you are doing, that everything else fades into non-existence." At the time, I fervently denied it, insisting that grooming is more like self-hypnosis, nothing to do with meditation. When this very good friend of mine piped up: "You haven't got a clue what meditation is, do you?" I ignored her and continued grooming the Duke, who by that time was melting into a pool of utter bliss.

Her words did make me think, though.

Fine. What IS meditation? I thought I had better look it up as I am supposed to be this highly-qualified stress management expert. More and more of my contemporaries were suggesting that meditation may well be a very effective antidote to the damage stress can do to sufferers' mental and physical health. According to Merriam-Webster, mediation is about "spending time in quiet thought for religious purposes or for relaxation," and to meditate is to "engage in contemplation or reflection" and "to engage in mental exercise (as concentration on one's breathing or repetition of a mantra) for the purpose of reaching a heightened level of spiritual awareness." Well, all those big words weren't particularly helpful.

Wikipedia was a bit more useful: "Meditation is a practice in which an individual train the mind or induces a mode of consciousness, either to realise some benefit or for the mind to simply acknowledge its content without becoming identified with that content." Right, but how would that benefit the person who is doing the meditation? How will it work for me, here on the farm, looking after the horses? How will it benefit people with sky-high stress-levels?

In this chapter, to help us understand what meditation is, we are going to look at

1. The definition of Meditation
2. The benefits of Meditation

You may have bought this book because you are interested in meditation as a stress management technique. For you, I have included a Stress Quiz at the end of this chapter. The quiz will help you find out how stressed you are right at this moment. Once you have established a meditation practice, you can take the quiz again and use it to measure the effectiveness of meditation as a stress management method.

1. Clarifying Definitions

Let's get some insights from a couple of experts:

"Meditation connects you with your soul, and this connection gives you access to your intuition, your heartfelt desires, your integrity, and the inspiration to create a life you love." Sarah McLean

"Meditation is not a way of making your mind quiet. It's a way of entering into the quiet that's already there – buried under the 50,000 thoughts the average person thinks every day." Deepak Chopra

"Loving-kindness towards ourselves doesn't mean getting rid of anything. It means we can still be crazy after all these years. We can still be angry after all these years. We can still be timid, jealous or full of feelings of unworthiness. The point is not to try to throw ourselves away and become something better. It's about befriending who we are already." Pema Chodron

"Some people think that meditation takes time away from physical accomplishment. Taken to extremes, of course, that's true. Most people, however, find that meditation creates more time than it takes." Peter McWilliams

"Dedicating some time to meditation is a meaningful expression of caring for yourself that can help you move through the mire of feeling unworthy of recovery. As your mind grows quieter and more spacious, you can begin to see self-defeating thought patterns for what they are, and open up to other, more positive options." Sharon Salzberg

Are you starting to get a better idea of what meditation is? If you are still not altogether clear, do not worry about it. It took me a few years to figure it out too. The best way to understand what meditation is and experience the benefits it can bring is...yes, you have guessed it. You need to start meditating. Try the first method that appeals to you. People often try traditional sitting meditation and unable to keep it up, give up on meditation altogether. Before you give up, try a couple of different methods. Choose one of the methods described in this book. Few people know that you can also meditate while you are walking, writing and working. One of these may work for you. Many people insist that they do not have enough time to meditate. Like I did, initially. Few know that only ten minutes a day can already help them cope with stress much more effectively.

2. The benefits of Meditation

- Better Impulse Control

Just to prove my friend wrong, I did some research. I googled "meditation" and "benefits of meditation." As you do. I discovered that meditation is simply the process of quieting our mind by focusing on a specific object (a burning flame), a sound (mantra or music) or an activity (breathing, writing, walking or working). One thing stuck in my already vastly overcrowded brain. Something that could work for me personally. Apparently, meditation can help you with impulse control (I do rather tend to fall back on terminology I picked up while studying psychiatry, my sincere apologies.) In other words, it can help you to think before you act. It can help you to acknowledge an emotion – like anger, frustration, impatience, hurt, humiliation and so on - without immediately reacting to it. This I could use. Definitely. But what proof exists that it actually works?

- Improved Concentration

Apparently, some time ago, a neuroscientist at the University of Arizona enrolled 45 human resource managers in a trial: a third took eight weeks of mindfulness-based meditation training, a third took eight weeks of body relaxation training and the rest had no specific training. All three groups were given "stressful multi-tasking" tests before and after the eight-week period. Those in the mindful-meditation group were able to sustain their focus for longer than those in the other groups. They also reported feeling less stressed. Interesting.

Less stress would be good, very good. Richard Davidson, another neuroscientist and founder of the Centre for Investigating Healthy Minds refers to the neurological effects of meditation as "rewiring the brain."

- Anti-ageing Influence

Most of the time, he says, "our brains are constantly being shaped by the forces surrounding us of which we are not aware or only very dimly aware." Research now suggests that people who meditate regularly are less at the mercy of these external forces and can, on the contrary, intentionally control this process. I liked the sound of that. No one likes to be at the mercy of forces beyond their control. In 1980, there were just three papers published on meditation. By 2014, there were 535. Now there are more than 6000. One found that people who practice meditation appear to lose less grey brain matter over time than their non-meditating counterparts. Another suggested regular meditation may "reduce the cognitive decline associated with normal ageing." A third, from 2012, found that long-term meditators may develop more folds in the brain cortex, which is associated with faster mental processing. A fourth found evidence of increased thickness in the areas of the brain associated with attention and awareness of sensations and the interpretation of emotions in oneself and others. (see Bibliography for more details about the studies)

The usually peacefully-sleeping scientist in me woke up. I looked at meditating a bit more closely. I was especially interested in mindfulness meditation: training our brains to not react immediately on impulse, without thinking. When something happens that presses our buttons, we often react without thinking. This sort of behaviour can quickly become a habit which means our minds will react in exactly the same way the next time a similar, let's say stressful scenario arises. Oops. Before we know it, we have said something we regret already, or smoked the cigarette we swore we would never smoke again, or eaten a whole bag of cream cakes, or gone on a shopping spree or sent an un-retractable e-mail - and a situation that initially was mildly stressful has now spiralled out of control.

- Effective Stress Management Technique

We get overwhelmed by the challenges and demands of our daily lives. I do, from time to time. This can lead to increased stress that can ultimately affect our mental and physical health. Using meditation on a regular basis gives our mind a chance to quiet itself and adjust to the stress that is part and parcel of modern life.

Initially, it was only to prove my friend wrong and to find out if it really can help with impulse control, that I took up meditation. As time went by, I realised what an effective stress management technique meditation really is. I have made it my life's mission to help people deal with stress, first as a medical doctor and now as a writer and a workshop presenter.

Stress Quiz

One of the very reasons you bought this book may have been to discover how to manage stress better. You are stressed. I know the feeling. But how stressed are you? To find out, you may want to take the quiz below. Allocate a number to each other these statements according to how accurately the statement applies to you:

- 0 = Not at all
- 1 = Just a little
- 2 = Somewhat
- 3 = Moderately
- 4 = Quite a lot
- 5 = Very much

1. I suffer regularly from headaches and/or migraines
2. I often feel sad for no apparent reason and I sometimes have dramatic mood swings.
3. I sometimes drink too much alcohol
4. I struggle to fall asleep. I often have nightmares. I wake up feeling tired.
5. I constantly feel pressurised to finish my work. I am forgetful and irritable.
6. I can't find the time to enjoy the simple pleasures of life
7. I do not enjoy social interaction, making an effort seems too much trouble.
8. I am dissatisfied with my work. I can't concentrate. I work hard but accomplish little.
9. My work is boring and monotonous.
10. My life seems pointless
11. I set myself unrealistic deadlines
12. I have to work longer and harder to achieve the same as before.
13. I am either overeating or I have entirely lost my appetite.

14. I always say 'yes' when I am asked to do something, either at work or at home.
15. I rigidly stick to my routine.
16. I clench my jaw and grind my teeth.
17. I have feelings of self-loathing.
18. I sometimes think of suicide.
19. I often feel guilty.
20. I find it hard to make decisions.

Stress levels:
- 0-20 Very low
- 21-40 Low
- 41-60 Moderate
- 61-80 High
- 81-100 Very High

If your stress level is anything more than twenty, you could benefit from meditation.

Religious Connections

I found out that sometimes even OM meditation can enable you to reach a higher state of consciousness, a "heightened level of spiritual awareness." According to the experts, meditation can enable you to connect to your deepest inner self and to the divine force within each and every one of us. Some people believe that praying is a meditation method. I realise that many people had some very specific ideas about the religious connotations of meditation. Some people think that people who meditate are involved with some or other sort of religion (sometimes they are.) They promptly decide that this is not for them. When I researched this assumption, I found that nearly all religions, including Christianity, practice some form of meditation. I also discovered that a large number of people who meditate are not religious at all.

Equine-facilitated Mindfulness Meditation

I would like to introduce my horse Belle de la Babinière. My soul sister, meditating. Usually, when she meditates, she also eats. She eats the whole day long and most of the night too, that is why her belly looks like a wine barrel. I do not recommend that you follow her example, as far as the eating part of her meditation is concerned. Eating mindfully, however, I am in favour of 100%. Belle eats simplemindedly mindfully. She examines every blade of grass in minute detail before she bites it off and chews carefully, for a very long time, before she swallows. I have thus come to the conclusion that Belle mindfully meditates 24/7 if left alone in her paddock. Until our ex-stallion Bass, a drop-dead-gorgeous Irish cob with a roguish streak, walks by.

There you are. Now we both know more about meditation. What I would like to say to you here and now - and I am sure that Belle will echo my sentiment - is to just go for it! Meditation will help you identify the procrastinating, forgiving, confused, understanding, worried and passionate person you already are. It will open door after door to further enjoyment of life, enchantment with who you are and enlightenment, for your own benefit and for the benefit of all sentient beings. A good starting point would be to choose a focused attention meditation method that focuses on compassion, kindness, empathy, tenderness and dedication to becoming the best person you can possibly be.

From Chapter 4 onward, I will explain how to do the specific meditation covered by that chapter. Before we go there though, let's find out a bit more about mindfulness, this state of mind my horses own so effortlessly.

Chapter 2

What is Mindfulness?

"Mindfulness is the aware, balanced acceptance of the present experience. It isn't more complicated than that. It is opening to or receiving the present moment, pleasant or unpleasant, just as it is, without either clinging to it or rejecting it." Sylvia Boorstein

I chose this quote to start this chapter as I really could not have said it better myself. My understanding of mindfulness is that it is all about being present in each moment. When we are present in the moment, and not distracted by what happened in the past or what may happen in the future, we have the opportunity to reflect and choose how we are going to react to a specific stimulus. We may choose to react in a way that will reduce our stress or in a way that will increase our stress. This is so incredibly empowering, don't you think?

To understand mindfulness better, in this chapter we are going to look at
1. The definition of Mindfulness
2. The effectiveness of Mindfulness
3. The difference between Mindfulness and Concentration
4. The implementation of Mindfulness
5. The benefits of Mindfulness
6. Best books about Mindfulness
7. Mindfulness and Meditation

1. The best definition of Mindfulness

Mindfulness is nothing new. Not being mindful is a bad habit that has existed for many centuries. Prof Jon Kabat-Zinn explains, "The habit of ignoring our present moments in favour of others yet to come leads directly to a pervasive lack of awareness of the web of life in which we are embedded. This includes a lack of awareness and understanding of our own mind and how it influences our perceptions and our actions. It severely limits our perspective on what it means to be a person and how we are connected to each other and the world around us." He is SO good at this. I wish I could say things with that amount of clarity and precision.

2. How does it work?

Mindfulness can be a very effective antidote to the "tunnel vision" that we often develop in challenging situations. Prof Mark Williams confirms "It's easy to stop noticing the world around us. It's also easy to lose touch with the way our bodies are feeling and to end up living 'in our heads' –caught up in our thoughts without stopping to notice how those thoughts are driving our emotions and behaviour. An important part of mindfulness is reconnecting with our bodies and the sensations they experience. Another important part of mindfulness is an awareness of our thoughts and feelings as they happen moment to moment. Awareness of this kind doesn't start by trying to change or fix anything. It's about allowing ourselves to see the present moment clearly. When we do that, it can positively change the way we see ourselves and our lives. Mindfulness also allows us to become more aware of the stream of thoughts and feelings that we experience and to see how we can become entangled in that stream in ways that are not helpful. This lets us stand back from our thoughts and start to see their patterns. Gradually, we can train ourselves to notice when our thoughts are taking over and realise that thoughts are simply 'mental events' that do not have to control us. Most of us have issues that we find hard to let go of and mindfulness can help us deal with these more productively." If you are as big a fan of quotes as I am, you will find several more informative and enlightening quotes about mindfulness at my blog.

Mindfulness enables us to be unconditionally present. Mindfulness is about paying non-judgemental attention to the details of our experiences. Being present, accepting the here and now, allows us to stop experiencing the unnecessary suffering that results from trying to escape or avoid all discomfort. Instead of struggling to avoid experiences that we find difficult to cope with, we practice being able to process these experiences. Interestingly, mindfulness can also be applied to enjoyable experiences. It is often just as difficult to hold onto enjoyable experiences as it is to endure unpleasant experiences. We expect that enjoyable experiences won't last and we desperately try to hold onto these experiences. Being mindful makes it easier to become fully engaged and savour the pleasant experiences as they occur.

3. Is it similar to Concentration?

Mindfulness and concentration are not the same thing. Ajahn Sumedho explains, "Some people do not know the difference between mindfulness and concentration. They concentrate on what they're doing, thinking that is being mindful. We can concentrate on what we are doing, but if we are not mindful at the same time, with the ability to reflect on the moment, then if somebody interferes with our concentration, we may blow up and get carried away by anger at being frustrated. If we are mindful, we are aware of the tendency to first concentrate and then to feel anger when something interferes with that concentration. With mindfulness, we can concentrate when it is appropriate to do so and not concentrate when it is inappropriate to do so." Mindfulness is a state of mind that enables us to maintain an open, accepting, non-judgemental focus.

As far as I am concerned, the main benefit of mindfulness is that it is a useful stress management technique. Effective stress management results in improved physical and mental health, although people who practice mindfulness often find that they are also less obsessed with what may go wrong in future or with regrets about what happened in the past. They are less focused on their own inadequacies and they are able to form deeper and more nourishing connections with others.

I have a lot of admiration for Prof Jon Kabat-Zinn, a biomedical scientist and founder of the Centre for Mindfulness in Medicine, Health Care and Society at the University of Massachusetts Medical School. He developed a mindfulness meditation method called Mindfulness-Based Stress Reduction (MBSR), to help patients cope with stress, pain, and illness through moment-to-moment awareness and is backed by a solid body of medical and scientific research. I have read most of his articles and books and I have based our workshops partly on the results of his research. You will find some of his articles listed in the Bibliography section of this book.

4. Implementing Mindfulness

If you want to incorporate mindfulness into your everyday activities, the easiest way to start would be to choose a task and to do it mindfully. While doing so, keep the following in mind:

- Do one thing at a time
- Read/listen carefully to instructions
- Divide a task into small easy-to-accomplish steps
- Give each step your full attention
- Allocate a specific time span to each step
- Undertake each step to the best of your ability
- Go for quality, not quantity

- If the steps are repetitive, develop a ritual
- Notice your progress step-by-step
- Be grateful for each step successfully completed
- Review your performance with each step
- Own your task
- Complete your task
- Note what you have learnt while doing this task
- Celebrate the completion of the task
- Take time out between tasks

Mindfulness Apps

You may want to try an app to help you implement mindfulness. Currently, the best-rated ones are (most available as Android and iPhone):

Headspace
Calm
Mindbody Connect
Mindfulness App
Smiling Mind
Meditation Timer Pro
Take a Break!
Breathe and Relax
Stop, Breathe and Think
Insight Timer

5. The Benefits of Mindfulness

A fair amount of research has been done about the benefits of meditation and of mindfulness. It seems that many of the benefits of meditation are also benefits of mindfulness. Some claims are purely anecdotal, others are fully backed by scientific research. I have made a list of the benefits backed by scientific research (see a list of the published articles in Bibliography):

Meditating regularly reduces feelings of anxiety, stress, depression, exhaustion, loneliness and irritability. Meditation reduces the production of stress hormones, so people who meditate regularly are calmer, more patient, happier and more content.

Meditation improves memory (working memory, creativity, attention span), it increases reaction speed and mental endurance.

Meditation enhances brain function. It increases grey matter in areas associated with self-awareness, self-control and attention. It promotes learning. It can even reduce some of the thinning of certain areas of the brain that naturally occurs with ageing. Mindfulness can slow the progression of age-related cognitive disorders, such as Alzheimer's dementia. It may also slow ageing at the cellular level by promoting chromosomal health and resilience.

Mindfulness increases patients' ability to cope with chronic pain.

Meditation boosts the immune system. People who suffer from cancer, for example, are admitted to hospital less often if they regularly practice meditation. Meditation can improve control of blood sugar in type II diabetes and improves heart and circulatory health by reducing blood pressure and lowering the risk of hypertension. Meditation reduces the risks of developing and dying from cardiovascular disease and lowers its severity should it develop.

Mindfulness improves sleeping patterns. Stress is one of the most common causes of insomnia. Mindfulness helps sufferers to calm down their minds and obsess less about what happened in the past or about what might happen in the future, allowing them to fall asleep and stay asleep.

Mindfulness builds happier relationships: Couples who actively practise mindfulness report that they are happier in their relationships. Couples still argue but are more likely to think before they respond. They are also more likely to take the effect of their response on their partner into account. The practice of mindfulness resolves stressful situations in relationships faster. Mindfulness increases empathy and compassion, not only in relationships between couples, but in all relationships.

Mindfulness reduces addictive and self-destructive behaviour. This includes alcohol abuse and the abuse of illegal and prescription drugs.

6. Best books about Mindfulness

A lot has been written in the last ten years about mindfulness: articles, blog posts and books. Some of the information presented is accurate and useful, some of it is confusing and unclear. I have listed the ten books that have helped me to understand what mindfulness is below, in case you would like to do some further reading.

Mindfulness for the Next Generation: Helping Emerging Adults Manage Stress and Lead Healthier Lives, by Holly Rogers. This very useful book helps parents explain mindfulness to their teenage children, thus providing them with an effective stress management strategy and starting them on the road to what will hopefully be a lifelong quest for personal development.

The Human Condition by Father Thomas Keating, a Trappist monk and priest, and known as one of the architects of Centering Prayer, a contemporary method of contemplative prayer, that emerged from St. Joseph's Abbey, Spencer, Massachusetts, in 1975. In his book, Father Keating discusses the contemplative tradition within Christianity. It is a good book if you are interested in contemplative meditation, whether you are a Christian or not.

Wherever You Go, There You Are: Mindfulness Meditation in Everyday Life by Jon Kabat Zinn. This is one of my favourite books by one of my favourite mindfulness authors. I appreciate Prof Kabat-Zinn's scientific approach. This book explains how to be mindful despite the stress, demands and obligations of our everyday lives.

Meditation for Beginners by Jack Kornfield. Meditation for Beginners shows you, step-by-step, how you can remain fully present in each moment.

The Power of Now: A Guide to Spiritual Enlightenment by Eckhart Tolle. Tolle's enthusiasm alone makes this an excellent book to read. It clearly and concisely explains the practice of "living in the now."

Coming to Our Senses: Healing Ourselves and the World Through Mindfulness by Jon Kabat Zinn This book is useful because it covers both meditation and mindfulness. The author shares his own experience. It takes a bit of time to work through, but once done, it becomes a valuable reference.

The Miracle of Mindfulness: An Introduction to the Practice of Meditation by Thich Nhat Hanh This book includes exercises and explanations about mindfulness – especially useful for beginners

How to Meditate: A Practical Guide to Making Friends with Your Mind by Pema Chödrön, a Tibetan nun

Meditation for Two by Dominic Barbier

8 Minute Meditation: Quiet Your Mind, Change Your Life by Victor Davich. This book is a beginner's guide to mindfulness. In the book, the author introduces a simple, user-friendly program to help beginners lower their stress levels in only eight minutes a day.

To make mindfulness even easier to understand and to use, I have gathered together what I think are the ten best ever TED talks about mindfulness in one blog post on my blog. In one of these talks, Andy Puddicombe, founder of Headspace, explains how putting everything down for ten minutes a day gives the brain a much-needed opportunity to rest and recharge its batteries. In another, Prof Jon Kabat-Zinn introduces mindfulness,

"Mindfulness practice means that we commit fully in each moment to be present; inviting ourselves to interface with this moment in full awareness, with the intention to embody as best we can an orientation of calmness, mindfulness and equanimity right here and right now. "In yet another, Susan Smalley and Diana Winston point out, "In practising mindfulness you are not trying to change who you are, but to become more fully present with your experiences...You may also become more discerning of your thoughts, feelings, and actions and that awareness will give you greater opportunity to make positive changes if you wish to do so." In one of the last talks, Ruby Wax, a stand-up comedian who has a Master's Degree in mindfulness-based cognitive therapy from Oxford, says mindfulness is like "going into the toilet, breathing, feeling my feet on the ground and my behind on the seat. It's about where your body is. And once you're in your body [instead of your mind] it all calms down."

7. The Relation between Mindfulness and Meditation

Prof Jon Kabat-Zinn, who has studied mindfulness for more than 35 years, says that mindfulness meditation is simply a specific method of meditation. I found out that there are several other meditation methods, like walking meditation, working meditation, writing meditation, music meditation, visualisation meditation etc. as well as the traditional sitting and breathing method of meditation. I never knew that you could meditate while you are moving around. Being a kinesthetic learner (more about this later,) the idea appealed to me. Especially if in addition to better impulse control, an effective stress management technique in itself, it could also help people relax and cope better with stress.

Equine-facilitated Mindfulness Meditation

A couple of years ago, I bought a new stallion, a heart-stoppingly handsome Irish cob called Baggio. Even though I have been mindfully meditating for many years now, and although I often manage to observe and distance myself from my thoughts and emotions before I react to them, Baggio showed me that I was nothing but an amateur in mindfulness meditation. Here was a breeding stallion, with at least 50 foals to his credit, and contrary to everything most people about stallions, thinks before he acts, even in the presence of mares. Those of you who know about horses, and stallions specifically, will understand why this is remarkable. Experienced breeders usually keep breeding stallions away from mares, until the time comes for them to breed. Baggio is a huge stallion, very powerful, there is no way I could keep him from breaking through the fencing and joining the mares should he decide to do that.

But Baggio has unshakable self-control. He stands in his paddock, next to the paddock of three very interested and undeniably willing Friesian mares, mindful of them at all times, without succumbing to his instinctive need to join them.

This is Baggio, the mindfully meditating stallion. Baggio, who stands quietly next to me, listening intently to my ramblings, who looks at me with those soft and understanding eyes, who thinks things over slowly and then agrees to walk to the school with me, up the alley between the fields with mares on both sides, without even looking in their direction. Talk about impulse control. This horse has so much to teach me. If you would like to meet this paragon of virtue, join us on a mindfulness meditation workshop here in the south of France!

"Direct your eye right inward, and you'll find a thousand regions in your mind yet undiscovered." Henry David Thoreau

In the next chapter, I will introduce you to the technique I use to help participants in our mindfulness meditation workshops choose the meditation method that will suit them best and that they will most easily be able to incorporate into their everyday lives.

Chapter 3

Choose Your Meditation Method

We are all different. We all have our own ideas and our own preferences. So have horses. Of the five horses we currently have on the yard, each has a very different personality, even though the mares are all Friesians and have a fair number of Friesian traits in common. When we do an equine-assisted personal development class, I ask each participant to choose a horse to help them with the task at hand. Within a day or two of the beginning of a Connect with Horses workshop, participants have already figured out which horse would be best for each individual task. The horses have also worked out what each participant will need help with. Sometimes, although a participant may choose one horse, another may insist on helping instead. Horses also have their own ideas and preferences. You can find out more about each horse on my website, EquineGuidedGrowth.com under "Her Mindfulness Mentors."

When I first started teaching meditation, I concentrated on traditional sitting meditation. I quickly discovered that although sitting meditation suited most of our workshop participants, it did not suit everyone. I remain convinced that mindfulness and meditation are highly effective stress management strategies, so I wanted all our participants to be able to benefit from practising meditation. Further research revealed that there is a huge variety of different meditation methods. The challenge was to find out which method would suit which practitioner.

I dug up my NLP books. I was looking for a test that would help me determine how to choose a meditation method for each participant. I found and tested a couple. Some were quite useless, others showed promise. I eventually chose Neil Fleming's VARK test, despite its imperfections, as it was useful to the largest number of participants.

In this chapter, you will learn more about the VAK model and how you can use it to choose the best meditation method for you. We will investigate

1. Neil Fleming's VARK test
2. The 4 Representational systems
3. The VAK Self-Assessment Quiz
4. How to choose the best meditation method for you

1. Neil Fleming's VARK test

In the 1970s, the idea that people learn in different ways became popular. Various learning style theories were formulated: David Kolb's model, Honey and Mumford's model, Anthony Gregorc's model, Neil Flemming's VAK/VARK model and several others. Many of these models influenced education despite the criticism that these models received from some researchers. Although there is ample evidence that people prefer to learn in different ways, few studies have found these learning styles models of use in education.

Neil Fleming's VARK model was built on the VAK model of Barbe and the representational systems (VAKOG) used in neuro-linguistic-programming. Fleming suggested that there are four ways of absorbing and interpreting new information:

Visual learning

Auditory learning

Read/write learning

Kinaesthetic learning

Fleming suggested that visual learners prefer to learn by seeing new information. He suggested that auditory learners learn through listening to lectures, discussions, tapes, etc. He suggested that tactile/kinaesthetic learners prefer to learn via practical experience—by moving, touching, exploring and experimenting. NLP proposes two further representational systems: olfactory (smell) and gustatory (taste). Neil suggested that students could use his learning model to identify their preferred learning style and so maximise their learning ability. Regretfully, this has not been confirmed in further research. Several further factors have to be taken into account.

Most people have a preferred primary way of learning. Depending on the circumstances, they might choose to use a secondary learning preference. A primary visual learner with a strong kinaesthetic secondary learning preference may use one or the other, depending on the learning challenge this person faces. Even though most people have a preferred mode of learning, we can all use all four ways of learning. Some people can use two ways of absorbing new information equally well. They are called multi-modals. Preferences may also change over time. To make matters even more complicated, learning preferences are also not the same as learning strengths. For example, you might be a good public speaker, but prefer to watch videos rather than to listen to auditory books.

These variants have made it difficult to study the effectiveness of the VARK model. I have found that identifying their preferred learning style, often reflected in the way they express themselves, has helped many of our participants to choose the meditation method that suits them best. It has helped them to understand how they experience and interpret events. It has also helped them to communicate more effectively. When they have used their thus identified communication presence in the sand school while interacting with the horses, the results were impressive.

People who prefer to learn by seeing new information, often express themselves in visual terms. They say, "I see what you mean." When we talk with other people, listening carefully, we can sometimes detect their preferred learning mode. This enables us to adjust the way we express ourselves to make it easier for them to understand us. It is also useful, when we work with a group of people, to make sure that we include all four learning styles in our speech or writing. This creates rapport between speakers and listeners, a technique that the advertising world has made very good use of.

2. The 4 representational systems

Whether you realise it or not, you have certain preferences as to how you absorb new information, how you analyse it, how you subsequently make decisions concerning this new information and how you then react to it:

Some people need to see what you mean before they can make decisions. They have a preference for visible or observed information: pictures, videos, diagrams, lists, demonstrations, displays, printouts, written directions, maps etc. They will say things like 'show me how you do it', 'let's have a closer look at this' and will learn quickest by reading instructions or by watching someone else perform a task.

Other people like to hear more about your ideas and make decisions based on how your ideas sound. These people prefer to absorb information and interpret experiences by listening: to the spoken word, to music, to sounds and to noise. They use phrases like 'tell me more', 'let's talk it over' and prefer to listen to instructions in person, over the telephone or by listening to a recording.

People who prefer to learn by reading or writing make a lot of notes and talk about "reading up about that" or "writing all this down." They are very keen list-makers. Many of them keep journals. Most are fast and ferocious readers.

Yet other people like to experience what you are talking about for themselves and then make a decision. Kinesthetic learners prefer new experiences to be physical. They prefer hands-on learning experiences. From them, you will hear phrases like 'let me have a try', 'how do you feel about this?' These are the people who like to experiment and who never look at the instructions first. Which accounts for all of us at some time or another!

These preferences can help you choose the perfect meditation method for you, one that will be easy to incorporate into your daily life.

To identify your preferred way of absorbing new information and interpreting experiences, I suggest you take Neil Flemming's VARK Questionnaire at the vark-learn.com website. This questionnaire includes the "reading and writing" learning style. I use a simplified version with our mindfulness meditation workshop guests: the VAK Quiz. It only takes about 10 minutes to complete. I include it below. Taking the quiz will give you three scores, one for each of Visual, Auditory and Kinaesthetic. The highest score is your preferred or dominant learning style. The order of your scores, e.g. AKV, is called your "VAK code".

3. The VAK Self-Assessment Quiz

Circle the answer that reflects your behaviour most often.
1. If I am choosing what I want to eat in a restaurant, I:
a) look around to see what other people are eating
b) discuss my options with the waiter
c) choose something I have eaten there before and that I know I like
2. When I need driving directions I usually:

a) consult a map - real or online

b) ask someone for directions

c) start driving in the general direction of the place that I am going to

3. When I cook a new dish, I like to:

a) follow a written recipe

b) phone the person who gave me the recipe

c) start putting ingredients together, tasting and adjusting as I go along

4. If someone asks me to teach them something new, I:

a) write down instructions, in detail

b) explain the process verbally

c) show them how to do it and then help them to get it right

5. I tend to say:

a) look how I do it

b) listen carefully

c) you have a go

6. During my free time I most enjoy:

a) going to the movies, watching TV or videos

b) listening to music or chatting to one of my friends

c) exercising or doing something creative

7. When I go shopping for clothes, before I try anything on, I tend to:

a) imagine how different pieces would look together

b) discuss it with the shop assistant

c) touch different pieces to determine the texture, weight and flexibility

8. When I am choosing a holiday I usually:

a) do a Google search, read travel blogs, visit websites with info about my destination

b) ask for recommendations from friends and discuss it with a travel agent

c) imagine, in detail, what it would feel like to be there

9. If I was buying a new car, I would:

a) first have a look at videos and read reviews online

b) first discuss what I need with various car salesmen

c) test-drive different models

10. When I am learning a new skill, I am most comfortable:

a) watching an instructor demonstrating the new skill first

b) discussing the procedure with the instructor

c) having a go at myself while the instructor helps me as I go along

11. When I use a new piece of equipment I usually:

a) read the instructions first

b) ask someone who has used it before for an explanation

c) get on with it, figuring it out as I go along

12. When I attend a concert:

a) I watch the musicians and the other people in the audience

b) close my eyes and listen to the music

c) some part of me will be moving in time to the music

13. I choose clothes or furnishings:

A) in my favourite colours

b) according to what other people (including the sales staff) say

c) according to how the piece of clothing or furniture feels when I touch it

14. When I am anxious, I:

a) see everything go wrong in my mind's eye

b) talk quietly to myself or out loud to someone else

c) can't sit still, I have to be in constant motion

15. When I have to revise for an exam, I generally:

a) write lots of notes, make lists, mind maps and diagrams

b) discuss what I am learning with other students

c) put what I have learnt into practice

16. I love:

a) watching videos, looking at photographs, admiring paintings or sculptures

b) listening to recordings, the radio or talking to friends

C) dancing/tennis/golf/running/walking/cycling, eating and drinking

17. When I first make contact for the first time, I usually:

a) arrange a face to face meeting

b) talk to the person on the telephone

c) get together and go for a walk

18. When I meet someone for the first time, I first notice:

a) the physical appearance of the person, eyes and hair colour, how the person is dressed

b) how they sound when they speak, if they have an accent or a speech impediment

c) their posture, how they are standing and how they move

19. If I am angry, I tend to:

a) keep replaying the event in my mind as if I am watching a film

b) speak up and out and tell people exactly how I feel

c) throw my toys out of the pram, literally

20. In my opinion, you can tell if someone is lying if:

a) they avoid eye contact

b) their voice changes, it rises or drops, becomes rough or too smooth or the rhythm changes

c) I get an uncomfortable feeling that they are

21. When I unexpectedly come across an old friend:

a) I say "it's lovely to see you after all this time!"

b) I say "it's great to hear your voice again!"

c) I give whoever it is a big hug

22. If I have to complain about something, I prefer to:

a) write a letter or an e-mail

b) pick up the phone and the discuss the problem

c) return whatever it is by post

Now add up how many A's, B's and C's you selected.

A's = B's = C's =

If you chose mostly A's you have a VISUAL perceptual preference.

If you chose mostly B's you have an AUDITORY perceptual preference.

If you chose mostly C's you have a KINAESTHETIC perceptual preference.

4. Choosing a meditation method to start with

Regretfully, this quiz is not fool proof. It is, however, very handy to help me decide which meditation method I should suggest a workshops participant should try first. You can do the same, using your results obtained by taking the VARK/VAK quiz. Interestingly, just taking the quiz often provides people with unexpected insights about themselves, helping them to make more appropriate choices.

Add to this the answers to the questions in the "preparation chapter."

1) What specific benefits are you looking for? For example, if you want to lower your stress levels, and
  - you are a visual learner, you may prefer to meditate while looking at the burning flame of a candle or by watching a guided visualisation meditation video on YouTube.
  - you are an auditory learner, you may prefer to listen to a guided meditation on YouTube with your eyes closed or you may prefer music meditation.
  - you learn by reading and writing, you may prefer to copy a loving-kindness meditation by hand. Just do a search for "loving-kindness meditation," and you will be able to choose from a variety of scripts.

If you are a kinesthetic learner, walking or working meditation may suit you best. Also on YouTube, you can find guided walking meditations, that you can listen to while you walk. More about this in the chapter about walking meditation.

While some people have a dominant learning style, other people have a mixture of two or less commonly, three learning styles. If you are one of the latter, you can try various meditation techniques until you find one that suits you best, at this time.

2) Which meditation method is of interest to you? In the chapters that follow, I discuss a number of meditation methods, always including what my horses taught me about the method. One of my own personal favourite meditation methods is working meditation. As I have a dominant kinaesthetic perceptual preference, I do working meditation while I am grooming the horses. There never seems to be enough hours in the day, so combining these two activities works very well for me. Chances are that you will find a method in this book that appeals to you and that you can incorporate into your life in the same way I added working meditation to my day. Of course, if you want to experience equine-guided meditation in person, you will have to join us here in the south of France! If you can't, don't worry, I will explain how to do equine-guided meditation without there being any horses present.

Have a look at your answers to the rest of the questions and commit to a practice that will work for you, that you can incorporate into your life, for the rest of your life. You can use the simple template below:
- Meditation method:
- VAK perceptual preference:
- Duration of each session:
- Time of the day you want to meditate:
- Duration of meditation: (Short of long-term)
- Keeping track: (journal/app like Insight Timer, Simple Habit or Stop, Breathe and Think)

You can now read the rest of the book, or you could read the chapter that focuses on the meditation method that you have chosen. As many people have more than one preferred learning style, it is worth reading the rest of the book as well, to find out if more than one meditation method appeals to you.

The first meditation method I want to tell you about is Writing Meditation - one of my all-time favourite meditation methods - probably not altogether surprising as I love writing. Chapter 4, the next one, also contains a discussion of mindful eating, as the first letter featured in this book is from a client who has weight management problems.

Chapter 4

Writing Meditation

Amanda's Letter

"Dear Dr Margaretha

I am at my wits' end. I have tried everything. I have tried every weight loss diet known to mankind. I have exercised, I have taken pills. I have been hypnotised, I have been coached...I have been through the mill so many times that I have long since lost count. I have been to slimming clubs. I have read mountains of weight loss books. The only thing I have not done is to lose weight permanently. Every time I try a new diet, I lose some weight. As soon as I stop the diet, I regain the weight I lost. In fact, I put more back on than I have lost. I am sure you have heard this sad story many times before. I am so tired of all this. My health is starting to suffer. I must find a way to lose weight forever!

I subscribed to your blog not long after you started blogging. I like your off-the-beaten-track sense of humour. One of your recent blog posts mentions mindful eating. I read up about it and my question to you today is this: Could mindful eating result in permanent weight loss? I no longer believe in quick weight loss diets. I have done my fair share of those. Diets make me ill because I do not get the vitamins and other essential nutrients I need while I am dieting. I am not one of those people who go around saying' "Oh, I barely eat a thing and the weight just keeps piling on!" That is not me. I love food and I eat a lot of it. I hate exercising and I avoid it whenever I can. I am interested in mindful eating because it sounds like something I could take on board. If I understand this correctly, mindful eating is about appreciating the food that one eats. It is about eating slower and thus eating less. I have to admit that I tend to wolf down a lot of what I eat mindlessly, especially when I am upset.

My unhealthy eating habits started after the birth of my first child. No, that is not correct. It started while I was pregnant with my first child. I wasn't particularly overweight as a child. I guess I would have been described as chubby. My mother loved food too. She loved cooking. Early on in my childhood, I learnt that eating and emotions were interconnected. We ate when we were happy. We ate when we were sad. We ate when we were frustrated and when we were bored. We ate because it was time for breakfast, lunch or dinner. We rarely ate because we were hungry. Chocolate featured prominently in my childhood. We had sugar with and in everything. Even so, I was not grossly overweight as a child. I was an active child. I love sports at school. I probably burnt off a fair amount of the calories I consumed.

My first pregnancy was a difficult one. I developed high blood pressure. My doctor worried about pre-eclampsia. I was told to take things easy. I spent most of the third trimester in bed. To make matters worse, I ate for the proverbial two. I put on three times as much weight as I should have. After my daughter's birth, things did not get any better. She had colic. She screamed for twenty hours out of every twenty-four. I got post-natal depression. I ate to make myself feel better. As you can see, I do understand how all this happened, I just do not know what to do about it. I did have some cognitive behavioural therapy, but it did not make a lasting impression on me.

Things did not improve once I got over the post-natal depression. I got pregnant with my son not long after. The weight just continued to pile on. An acrimonious divorce followed two years later. As a single mother with two children under five, I had more pressing worries that my weight. My stress levels were sky-high. I ate to relieve the stress. A very bad stress management strategy, as it turned out. Even so, I stuck to this strategy faithfully in the difficult years that followed.

Carrying around the extra weight damages more than my health. My self-image is also in shreds. I have next to no confidence in myself. Once again, I have to correct myself. I do have some confidence in myself. I have always been good at my job. You have probably guessed it, I am a chef. I love working with food. I am at my happiest when I am creating new dishes. I love watching people's faces when they first taste my masterpieces. The compliments that come my way inspire me to create more mouth-watering concoctions. The problem is, my job makes it nearly impossible for me to stick to any diet. I have to taste the food that I prepare. I am constantly surrounded by food. I constantly think about food. I dream about food. I think I can say, with conviction, that I am obsessed with food.

I read your book, Confidence made Simple: 16 French Women's Confidence Secrets. I found the chapter "Sumptuous Self-care" enlightening. Here were principles I could apply to my life. The French approach to food and eating resembles my own approach. They love food. So many people, when they go on a diet, convince themselves that they hate food. I could never do that.

With all this in mind, I think I would like to find out how this mindful eating concept works. My idea is not to lose weight while I am doing your workshop (that would truly be a miracle!) but to learn more about mindful eating. I am absolutely fascinated by the French Paradox. I cannot understand how French people seem to be able to eat unbelievably rich food and drink copious amount of wine without putting on weight. That they also manage to live long and healthy lives seems grossly unfair.

I would like to make a reservation for the July workshop. I am not particularly interested in sitting meditation, but if you think it would be useful to me, I am willing to give it a go. Also, I have to warn you, I am scared witless of horses, due to an unfortunate incident in my childhood.

All the best
   Amanda."

Assessing Amanda's problem

When I received Amanda's application, I was delighted. I have a lot of experience working with women who want to lose weight. Amanda's honest e-mail, full of insight and self-knowledge, made it clear that mindful eating could be extremely beneficial to her. I looked forward to meeting her. I was keen to introduce her to a weight management strategy that might just change her life. I suspected that she was already half-way there. She knew how to appreciate food, she probably just needs to eat slower and adjust her portion sizes. She also needed to find a more efficient way to cope with stress.

I suspected that Amanda was primarily a gustatory learner. Testing confirmed my suspicion. This came as no surprise. Most chefs are. She quickly mastered the art of mindful eating. In my mind, mindful eating is about being fully present in the moment when you are eating. When you eat mindfully, you use all five your senses to appreciate the food you have chosen. Being present in the moment allows you to slow down and notice what you are putting in your mouth. You can make better choices. Mindfulness can help you to avoid stuffing yourself with whatever there is to hand because you are stressed.

Mindfulness helps us to notice and distance ourselves from self-critical or guilty thoughts while we are eating.

We talked about using all five of our senses to appreciate food and not just our sense of taste and our sense of smell. As a chef, Amanda was already familiar with this practice. She already used her senses of sight, smell and taste with great expertise. We added her sense of hearing and her sense of touch. She had a marvellous time at a weekly fresh fruit market in a neighbouring village. She spent the whole morning touching, smelling, tasting and looking at the large variety of fruit, vegetables, cheeses, charcuterie and bread typical of our region. She was clearly in her element. She talked to the stall owners. I translated. The language barrier meant that she had to listen attentively. If the market did not close at twelve o'clock, she would probably still be there. She did learn two very important lessons that day. Firstly, she learnt how important it is to listen carefully. Not being an auditory learner, this did not come naturally to her. She learnt how much more you find out when you do take the time to really listen. It was an important lesson to learn, as I suspected she rarely listened properly. Especially not to her own body when it said, "I am not hungry anymore. I am full."

She also learned a thing or two about portion sizes. French market stall owners generously allow their clients to taste a variety of their products before making a purchase. This enables French cooks to, for example, choose the perfect cheese to compliment the dish they have in mind. The pieces of cheese offered to clients have to be small, or the market owners will not make a profit. Amanda insisted that the portions were way too small for her to be able to taste the cheese accurately. I pointed out that no one else seemed to have that problem. I also pointed out that intense discussions followed the tastings of said slivers. That day, Amanda realised she only needs a minuscule portion to enable her to precisely smell and taste food. She noted that tasting smaller portions while she was at work and being satisfied with smaller portions at home might go a long way to help her get rid of her unwanted kilogrammes.

Amanda added a wine tasting tour to her workshop and the experience re-enforced this idea. She discovered that she only needs a small sip to decide whether she likes a wine or not. She realised that spitting out the wine after tasting it not only helps professional wine tasters not to get drunk, it also helps them not to consume too many calories. Amanda envisioned not swallowing all the food she tastes while she is working either. This girl was serious about losing the excess weight she was carrying.

Another thing that Amanda took to with gusto was my suggestion of an early morning walk. She was up and ready to go every morning, without exception. She practised mindfulness while walking, paying particular attention to what her senses were telling her. One morning, after her walk we talked about the benefits of exercise as a stress management tool as well as a weight loss tool. Amanda said she had forgotten how much she enjoyed just being outside. She decided to walk to work in future, at least three times a week. Especially as she could walk through a lovely park on the way. We also discussed the possibility of using mindfulness to combat stress and lose weight. Mindfulness gives us the opportunity to stop in the moment and decide whether we really want another doughnut. It also offers us the chance to react in a stress-reducing way when we find ourselves in challenging situations.

Amanda had a lot of questions about mindful eating. Mindful eating was the subject of one of my blog posts in November 2016. I include it here because it explains exactly what mindful eating is.

Adjusting Amanda's approach to food: Mindful Eating

"Thanksgiving is just around the corner, which means roast turkey with chestnut truffle stuffing, home-made cranberry sauce, mashed potatoes with Parmesan cheese, maple-glazed carrots with pecan nuts, green bean casserole with bacon, cast-iron skillet cornbread, caramelised sweet potatoes and a pumpkin pie with a walnut crust. We do not celebrate Thanksgiving here in France. Our festive seasons starts with Saint Nicholas, on the sixth of December. St Nicholas is followed by the traditional Christmas Reveillon dinner on the 24th. Next is the New Year's Eve Reveillon on the 31st: a feast that starts around ten o'clock on New Year's Eve and continues to at least five o'clock the next morning. Our festive season ends with Epiphany, on the sixth of January, a full month after the start of the season on the sixth of December.

Most of us will eat a substantial amount of food and drink much more than we usually do, during the next month. Many of us will also put on a substantial amount of weight. Reflecting on this seemingly-unavoidable outcome, I thought I should write a post about mindful eating. My aim with this blog post is to empower you not to wake up on the seventh of January feeling like a stuffed pig with several unwelcome pounds of fat determinedly clinging to you in all the most unwanted places.

Mindful eating can help you avoid this unsavoury experience. I am not making this up. There is solid scientific evidence that backs up this statement. At the start of yet another holiday season characterised by decadently delicious and impossible-to-resist delicacies, you may want to take an in-depth look at the concept of mindful eating. Why? Because mindful eating will help you:
- fully appreciate and savour everything you eat,
- avoid eating and drinking so much that you end up feeling like an over-stuffed sausage,
- get to January with having put on a single pound.

What is mindful eating, aka mindfulness-based intuitive eating?

Mindful eating is not about dieting. It has absolutely nothing to do with the deprivation that characterises most diets. Mindful eating is about celebrating food. It is about rejoicing in the enjoyment that lovingly prepared food and expertly produced wine can give us. During the holiday season, mindful eating is also about sharing home-made and often home-grown favourites with our friends and family, our nearest and dearest. Mindful eating is something that we have been doing in France for many centuries.

Mindful eating is about paying attention to what you are eating. When you eat mindfully, you concentrate on and savour every sensation you experience while eating a melt-in-the-mouth bite or drinking a never-to-be-forgotten sip.

What are the benefits of mindful eating?

Mindful eating can help you to feel better about your body because mindful eating also involves non-judgemental awareness. It can help you lose weight, keep the weight off, manage pre-diabetes/diabetes and cope with chronic eating disorders.

How does one eat mindfully?

It is very simple. To ensure that not a single taste-sensation escapes you, you have to use all five your senses while you are eating and drinking.

- Sight: Start by looking closely at what you are eating. Notice the various elements that your meal consists of. Try to guess what each bite is going to taste like, by looking at it. Does the turkey look over-cooked, under-cooked or roasted to perfection? Has it been glazed? Any visible indication of what it has been glazed with? What is the colour of the cranberry sauce? Light red, copper red, plum-red or dark red? How might the colour affect the taste? What does the mash look like? Light and airy or thick and creamy? How did the chef cut the carrots? Rounds or sticks? Pay attention to the shapes, colours and textures of the food in front of you. Notice how you respond to the sight of all this scrumptious-looking food. Does your mouth start to water? Are you looking forward to your first bite? What do you love and what do you prefer to avoid?

- Smell: Pay careful attention to the aromas that you can smell. Can you smell any garlic? Onions? Rosemary? Thyme? Does what you see and what you smell complement each other? Can your nose help you guess what each bite is going to taste like? Any aromas that clash, or that you do not like?
- Hearing: What do you hear? People may be chatting excitedly around you. Festive music may be playing in the background. You may hear a champagne cork pop. If you bring your champagne glass to your ear, you may be able to hear the bubbles bursting.
- Taste and Feel: Go on, take your first bite. Pay attention to the texture and the feel of the food in your mouth. Listen to the sound it makes when you chew. Is it crunchy? Smooth and creamy? Of what exactly does it taste? Can you identify the various flavourings? How salty is it? How sweet? Or is it tart, like the cranberry sauce? Too tart? Does it taste homemade? What does it remind you of? How does it compare with last year's turkey? Chew slowly and savour each bite.
- Swallow: Pay attention to the sensation of swallowing. Are you swallowing too much at once? Do you swallow before you have finished chewing? Are you starting to feel full? If you are starting to feel full, put your knife and fork down. You do not need to feel obliged to drink or eat more than you want. You do not have to eat something that you do not like.

Non-judgemental Awareness

Be mindful of the thoughts that pop into your head. You may notice that you are eating more than you want because you do not want to hurt your hostess's feelings. You may notice that you are eating too fast and drinking too much. You may become aware that you feel intimidated about eating in front of other people. You may notice that you feel obliged to eat to eat something that you do not want. Mindful eating means that you notice these thoughts, but you do not engage with them. You do not have to start beating yourself up because you are eating for the wrong reasons. You do not have to have a go at yourself for eating or drinking too much.

Not engaging emotionally with your thoughts enables you to look at them objectively and to choose how you are going to react. You can choose to make yourself miserable for the rest of the evening. Or you can choose to eat and drink more mindfully from that moment on.

You can choose to do one thing at a time. You can choose to stop eating or drinking while you are listening or taking part in the conversation. When you are eating, you are eating mindfully. When you are listening, you are listening attentively. When you are talking, you are giving the conversation your full attention. Find out what other people think of a dish, what flavourings they have noticed. French people do this a lot. It is great fun to try and guess the exact ingredients, seasonings and flavourings that the cook has used. If you particularly enjoy something, pay it forward and pass on your compliments to the cook.

When you are eating mindfully, you tend to eat and drink more slowly. You have time to pay attention to how your body is feeling. You notice when you are starting to feel full. When you eat mindfully, you often eat and drink substantially less than you would when you are eating mindlessly.

You may also notice that you are, in fact, not hungry at all, that you are eating because you are feeling stressed. You may realise that eating is not helping you feel less stressed. You may decide to use a different stress management strategy.

Eating mindfully enables you to appreciate what you are eating and drinking. You appreciate all the work that went into the production of the food. You realise how grateful you feel to everyone involved in providing you with this food: from the farmer who sowed the seed to the waiter who put the plate down before you."

At its most essential, the apple you hold is a manifestation of the wonderful presence of life. It is interconnected with all that is. It contains the whole universe; it is an ambassador of the cosmos coming to nourish our existence. It feeds our body, and if we eat it mindfully, it also feeds our soul and recharges our spirit. Thich Nhat Hanh.

Amanda's meditation method: Mindful Writing Meditation
   Amanda has 4 options:
   1. The Loving-Kindness Meditation script
   2. Free-writing with prompts
   3. Writing Letters
   4. Keeping a Meditation Journal

Amanda agreed with all this, in principle, but she felt that her bad habits were so entrenched that she was not sure how useful this technique would be to her, on its own. She felt she needed something more. I suggested writing meditation. Amanda's secondary learning preference was the reading/writing learning style, according to her VARK test. I also chose writing meditation for Amanda, because I was convinced that to be effective, Amanda would need a meditation method that would keep both her mind and her hands busy. It also had to be a meditation method that did not resemble traditional meditation. She clearly stated in her e-mail that she was not interested in the traditional method of sitting meditation.

I explained to Amanda that meditation is a state of heightened mental awareness and inner peace that brings mental, physical, and spiritual benefits. I pointed out that meditation can be practised without adherence to any religion or philosophy.

Amanda said that, for her, meditation conjures up an image of a hermit sitting on a mountaintop, for hours, in the lotus position, eyes closed and in silence. She was surprised to find out that meditation can also be practised while walking, chanting, working in the garden or writing at a desk. She was relieved to discover that meditation can be beneficial even if only practised for a few minutes a day. Amanda felt she could manage to incorporate 10 minutes of writing meditation into her day.

1. The Loving-Kindness Meditation script

To help Amanda understand writing meditation, I talked to her about focused meditation and about insight meditation. During focused writing meditation one concentrates on a something specific, like copying a script. During insight writing meditation, you attend without attachment or aversion to whatever thoughts, feelings and sensations you experience and then you write these down. The writing meditation method I felt would most benefit her was focused writing meditation.

Copying a script, for example, a loving-kindness script, can re-program our subconscious much more effectively than if you were simply reading, hearing or reciting the words – and with very little conscious effort on your part.

If you too find traditional sitting meditation difficult, writing gives your busy mind something to do as you cultivate awareness of the overall experience. Focused writing meditations not the same as thera-peutic writing or writing therapy. The latter would qualify as insight writing meditation. Therapeutic writing differs from focused writing meditation. Therapeutic writing involves writing about a specific emotionally charged episode. The aim is to arrive at a therapeutic outcome, whereas the aim of focused writing meditation is purely to meditate, to familiarise oneself with the practice of meditation or to try a different type of meditation.

Writing meditation is an easy meditation method to master. All you have to do is find a quiet spot where you will not be disturbed, take a few deep breaths and write. We usually introduce our workshop participants to four different writing meditation methods. One of the easiest ways to do writing mediation is by copying a loving-kindness script.

Start with yourself, since we often have difficulty loving others without first loving ourselves. Sitting quietly, write slowly and steadily, the following phrases:
   May I be filled with loving-kindness.
   May I feel connected, calm and contented.
   May I accept myself just as I am.
   May I be happy.
   May I know the natural joy of being alive.

While you write these phrases, allow yourself to thoroughly absorb their meaning.

Now think of someone whom you care about, who means a lot to you and who has always been supportive of you. A friend, a family member, your significant other. Bring this person to mind as vividly as you can, and reflect on his/her good qualities. Repeat the exercise above by writing the following phrases:
   May you be filled with loving-kindness.
   May you feel my love now.
   May you accept yourself just as you are.
   May you be happy.

May you know the natural joy of being alive.

Do the same with a "neutral" person, someone you do not particularly like or dislike. A colleague, maybe. Finally, repeat the exercise while thinking of someone you actually dislike. Next, repeat the exercise with all four of these people together — yourself, your friend, a neutral person and the person you actively dislike. Finally, extend your feelings to everyone around you, to everyone in your neighbourhood, in your city, your country, and the rest of the world.

You will find various Loving Kindness Meditation Scripts online, just do a loving-kindness script search.

2. Free-writing with prompts

Another option is to write about whatever comes into your head for a set amount of time. If nothing comes into your head, you can use one of these prompts:

The happiest/proudest/saddest/most embarrassing moment of my life was when...

My favourite way to spend the day is...

If I could talk to my teenage self, I would say to myself...

Make a list of 30/50/100 things that make you smile...

The best night of my life so far was...

I would like to be remembered for...

I am grateful for...

The worst thing I ever did...

My childhood was characterised by...

The highlights of last week were...

In 10 words, I would describe myself as...

I felt most alone in my life when...

The most important lessons I have learnt in my life are...

I struggle with...

I really look forward to...

I really wish others knew this about me...

Before my next birthday, I would like to accomplish...

The best relationship I have had so far was...

If money was not an issue, I would...

The relationships that matter most to me are...and I maintain and improve them by...

I have changed and grown in the last year by...

The most daring or scariest thing I have ever done was when...

The most appropriate gift I have ever received was...

The hardest decision I have ever made was...

If I had one day to do over and over, I would want to...

The best advice I have ever received that encouraged me to follow my dreams was...

My favourite thing about being a woman (or a man) is...

The personality traits I admire in others and would like to acquire myself are...

I always put off...

The best holiday I have ever had was...

I have decided today to apologise to...

I wish I could...

The last time I was up all night...

My favourite poem is...

If I wrote a book/movie/song it would be about...

3. Writing Letters

A third possibility is to write a letter as writing meditation. These days, people rarely write each other letters. We write e-mails, send texts, chat on Messenger or on WhatsApp...I wonder, does anyone still write love letters and send them by post? And if not, why not? A letter sent by post can convey so much. Especially if read mindfully. There is the paper the letter is written on: the colour, the texture, the watermark, the thickness, the sound the paper makes when pulled from the envelope, the rustling of the pages as they are turned. There is the handwriting, the colour and quality of the ink, the type of pen used to write with. Might there be a whiff of some exotic perfume when the letter is opened? There is also the envelope, the choice of stamp and the care with which the letter was addressed. So much information in such a small package...and all that long before one has read the first word.

I love letters written by hand and sent by post, especially love letters. As you may have guessed, the writing/reading learning preference features prominently in my VARK profile. There is a specific type of love letter that I encourage workshop participants with strong writing/reading preferences to write - a love letter to yourself. At least once in their lifetime, but preferably more often than that.

Towards the end of the workshop, I decided to address Amanda's perceived lack of self-confidence and suggested that she might want to write such a letter to herself. I encouraged her, "Write a letter to yourself. A letter of understanding, acceptance and appreciation. A letter to yourself, celebrating your talents, your achievements and your victories. A letter to the person in the mirror, telling her what you admire and appreciate about her. A letter full of empathy and never-wavering support. If you would rather, write a compassionate letter to your younger self or to yourself at the end of your life."

Kristen Neff, the author of the book "Self-Compassion - Stop Beating Yourself Up and Leave Insecurity Behind" and the creator of the Self-compassion Scale says, "I found in my research that the biggest reason people aren't more self-compassionate is that they are afraid they'll become self-indulgent. They believe self-criticism is what keeps them in line. Most people have gotten it wrong because our culture says that being hard on yourself is the way to be."

In my book, You ARE good enough - a 10 step strategy to stop sabotaging yourself, I devote a whole chapter to self-compassion as most people who feel that they are not good enough are very good at self-criticism, but rarely practice self-compassion. In this chapter, I explain exactly how to go about it, as I feel it is such an important aspect of self-care.

I found a video on YouTube that illustrates this point. A group of women are asked to write down the comments that they make to themselves about their bodies during the day. Two actresses then repeated these comments, in a restaurant, to each other. Several women nearby, hearing this, interrupted the actresses, to object at the way they spoke to each other. The irony is that this is exactly the way we speak to ourselves, most days. We cannot bear to hear this said out loud, to another woman, but we persist in berating and criticising ourselves in this way.

No wonder Kristin Neff and Christopher Germer, a leader in the integration of mindfulness and psychotherapy developed the MSC (mindful self-compassion) method. This approach appeals to me, not in the least because there is a solid body of research to back it up.

But what exactly is MSC? According to the developers, "mindfulness is the first step in emotional healing - being able to turn toward and acknowledge our difficult thoughts and feelings (such as insecurity, hurt, frustration, confusion) with a spirit of openness and curiosity. Self-compassion involves responding to these difficult thoughts and feelings with kindness, empathy and understanding so that we soothe and comfort ourselves when we're hurting."

When you write yourself a love letter, you are practising mindful self-compassion.

Amanda agreed that we spend so much time judging ourselves, criticising ourselves, blaming ourselves and beating ourselves up that it is not surprising at all that we suffer from low self-esteem. She agreed to write the letter. She said, "a healthy and realistic self-image and a few dollops of sustainable self-esteem could make my life so much easier. It will certainly help me cope with stress better!"

4. Keeping a Meditation Journal

While we are on the subject of writing meditation, as this sort of meditation seemed to work for Amanda, we talked about keeping a meditation journal. I explained she may want to do all her writing meditations in a journal. This way, she could also keep an eye on her progress. Every day, after her writing meditation, she may make a short note. One day she might write something like: Free-writing meditation. 10 minutes. Couldn't concentrate. Really struggled. Needed to use several different prompts. On another day, she might write something completely different: Didn't get home till two o'clock. 127 covers tonight. No time for writing meditation. Again. Will have to try morning meditation instead. And yet on another day: Copied loving-kindness meditation script. Very slowly. Felt completely relaxed and refreshed after. Amanda agreed that a meditation journal could motivate her to practice meditation regularly because she enjoys keeping records and measuring her progress. Record keeping is a very useful exercise, it can lead to insights that we may otherwise have missed.

Equine-facilitated Mindfulness Meditation

You may be wondering how Amanda got on with the horses. The short answer is: Splendidly. The more detailed answer is that she had very little choice in the matter. Our youngest horse, Aurore d'Alegria, took a shine to Amanda the first day Amanda arrived. This is not surprising, because Aurore, like Amanda, is a bon vivant who passionately loves her food. Aurore would come over at a canter whenever she saw Amanda, and although this initially scared the living daylights out of Amanda, she could not resist Aurore's enthusiasm indefinitely. Amanda managed to overcome her fear and approach Aurore, tentatively at first. Soon more boldly only to be showered with sloppy kisses as soon as Amanda came within reach. A solid friendship was born, which resulted in Amanda taking Aurore for walks to where she found the lushest, greenest grass during her morning walks. Amanda discovered that a fear once conquered, might turn into an unexpected blessing.

Talking about our workshops, you may have noticed on our website that we only host mindfulness meditation workshops. We also host three-in-one walking, wine tasting and writing workshops. We started these after I started writing. When I write, I sometimes get the all-this-has-been-said-before-I-don't-know-why-I-bother blues. Writers also call it writer's block.

Walking and Wine Tasting Workshop for Writers (and others)

When I am in serious need of inspiration, I take an afternoon off to walk a section of the Camino de Santiago pilgrim's route. It is nearly a thousand years old, give or take a few decades. It runs along the valley below our farm. I started doing this after I saw an interview with Paulo Coelho on YouTube. He said that he was inspired to write his first book 'The Pilgrimage' while walking the Camino.

I never paid much attention to the Camino before I started writing. I knew that hundreds of people walk the Camino every year. I have seen them in neighbouring towns and along the roads, blissed-out expressions on their faces and backpacks on their backs. Most of these people say that walking the Camino has been a life-changing experience. I always took that with a pinch of salt. I thought that is wasn't really my sort of thing even though people from all walks of life walk the Camino, whether they are religious or not. Several books have been written about the Camino and several films have been made about it.

It is just that I always had more important things to do. Until I started writing, that is. Until the first time I got stuck. There is something magical about walking along this ancient path, following in the footsteps of thousands of people before me. The Camino has never failed me. I have never walked the Camino without coming back to my computer motivated to start writing again. Walking the Camino has inspired me to create our "Walking and Wine Tasting Workshop for Writers." Writers with writer's block come and stay with us for a few days. They have the opportunity to walk the Camino. Most of them soon get their writing mojo back. No doubt the wine tasting part of the weekend also has something to do with their renewed enthusiasm...

Attending a walking and wine tasting workshop here in the south of France will enable you to get away from the hustle, bustle and never-ending demands of everyday life, allowing you to recharge your batteries, reconnect with nature, unwind and de-clutter your mind and increase your physical fitness. If walking the Camino de Santiago is on your bucket list but you are intimidated by the physical and mental demands of walking the full distance – these workshops offer you the opportunity to walk part of the Camino and experience the Camino first-hand: the easy camaraderie between walkers, the breath-taking scenery, the mood-lifting effect of following in the footsteps of walkers who have walked the Camino these last 900 years, sleeping along the way in an ancient French farmhouse, swimming in a private lake at the end of the walking day and sampling the excellent food and wine of the region.

In the next chapter I will introduce you to walking meditation – featuring several ways to enrich mindful walking meditation – and to my two walking meditation instructors: Aurore d'Alegria and Aurileo D'Alegria.

Chapter 5

Walking Meditation

Elsa's Letter

"Dear Dr Montagu,

I am writing to ask if I could possibly join you for the mindfulness meditation workshop of the 20-27th of July. My friend Anna Marsh, who attended one of your workshops last year, suggested that I give it a go. I have had a look at your website. I think that I would greatly benefit from attending a workshop based on mindfulness and meditation. I have always loved horses (although I have never had enough funds to realise my dream of owning a horse) and I have always wanted to visit France. I cannot think of a more enchanting place to spend a week than in the south of France!

If I told you a bit about myself, you will understand why your workshops appeal to me. I am a mother of two teenage boys. My eldest is fourteen, his brother is twelve. My husband and I divorced three years ago. It was not exactly amicable. Things have been difficult ever since. My job is stressful. I have to work long, irregular hours to provide for my boys. My husband contributes, but not in a particularly regular fashion. Financially we are managing, even if it is only just. I cannot for a single moment allow myself to think what would happen if I lost my job. I need to hold on to this job at all costs.

We live in a large city. My salary is sufficient for us to be able to rent an apartment in a decent if not a prosperous neighbourhood. My boys attend a good school, but they spend a large part of the day on their own. I have to work until eight o'clock every weekday evening. I often work later than that. I worry about them all the time. I know they are good boys, but there are so many temptations in a big city for boys of their age!

Lately, work has become more stressful than ever before. Our company is under threat of a hostile take-over. My boss is getting more and more demanding. Sometimes unreasonably so. There is a lot of tension in the office. I often agree to take on work that I do not have time for. I have always found it difficult to say 'No.' As work became more stressful, I have started to suffer from insomnia. I fall asleep, dead tired, only to wake up three or four hours later, wide awake and anxious. My health is now starting to suffer. I am not eating properly. I rarely have time to prepare and eat a proper meal. At weekends I do the shopping. I clean the apartment and I wash our clothes. I watch the odd television show with the boys. Sometimes I have a coffee with my girlfriends. I have little time to take care of myself.

In the few moments I do have to myself, I have been looking into mindfulness. Several of my friends and colleagues have found it useful as a stress management tool. I have tried meditation in the past, but I did not work for me. I just cannot sit still that long without starting to worry. I am sure it could help me. I have read a lot of about the benefits of meditation, if only I can make it work for me. This is why I am interested in your workshops. It says on your website that you introduce participants to a variety of different meditation techniques. Techniques that are especially useful to people who do not find traditional sitting meditation of much use. Well, that's me.

I must admit, despite my attraction to horses, I know very little about them. I have never had anything to do with them. In all honesty, although I love looking at pictures and videos of horses, in real life I think I will find them rather intimidating. Anna said she felt exactly the same before she attended your workshop. She said that she found the personal empowerment sessions with the horses invaluable, despite her initial fear. I have to admit, she is much more assertive since she has come back. I mostly need help with stress management, but I would also like to be able to stand up to my boss.

If you think the workshop would be right for me and you have a place left, please let me know. I need to ask for time off as soon as possible.

Looking forward to hearing from you,
  Elsa Watts."

Less than a decade ago, my life very much resembled that of Elsa's. Working as a medical doctor, I had a stressful job looking after stressed people. I started to think that stress was at the bottom of many of my patients' problems. I realised that stress prevention may be an effective way of avoiding many of the illnesses I saw in medical practice. To cut a long story short, when I discovered the health benefits of mindfulness and meditation, I decided that I wanted to host residential workshops helping people incorporate these benefits into their everyday lives. It is exactly because of women like Elsa Watts that I started the mindfulness and meditation workshops that we host here in the south of France.

Assessing Elsa's problem

Stress is part of modern-day living. We cannot avoid stress. A reasonable amount of stress can even be good for us. It helps us to perform at our best. We get into trouble when the stress we are subjected to becomes overwhelming. The specific level where stress becomes unmanageable varies from person to person. Person A may find a certain amount of stress unbearable, while person B does not even notice. It depends a lot on what else is going on in our lives. If we have to cope with stress at work as well as at home, we will feel stressed sooner than someone who has a peaceful home life. When stress continues over a period of time, even if it varies in intensity during that period, it can damage our physical and/or mental health. Elsa realised that she had to find a way to cope with stress before it did permanent damage to her health.

Elsa did indeed benefit from attending a workshop. She did not make it to the workshop in July. She could not manage to get time off until the September workshop. She arrived on a warm, late summer's afternoon. The air was fragrant with the perfume of our late-flowering Madame Alfred Carrière roses. She was neatly dressed but anxious and flustered. The airline had lost her luggage during the flight. She was upset and could barely manage to keep still for five seconds. She paced up and down in the front courtyard, wringing her hands, while I rang the airline to find out what had happened to her luggage. I could well understand that she would find sitting meditation a challenge.

Luckily, she was reunited with her luggage that very evening. Still, Elsa found it impossible to relax. She continued to fret, about the boys, about work and about the workshop. She couldn't decide whether coming to the workshop had been the right thing to do. That first evening, we all indulged in a full Gascon dinner. If I remembered correctly, we had Canard Confit (duck), a culinary speciality of Gascony. We had potatoes and mushrooms (cèpes) fried in duck fat and seasoned with a bit of garlic and parsley. We also ate home-grown, picked-that-afternoon green beans (haricots de Tarbes) with slices of chorizo sausage and tomato sauce. Dessert was a Croustade à l'Armagnac, a scrumptious, crisp and light apple tart typical of this region. We drowned it in liberal amounts of fresh, full-fat cream. We washed it all down with a glass or two of Madiran wine, as recommended by Prof. Roger Corder in his book

The Red Wine Diet, for its anti-ageing and health-giving properties.

Elsa felt much better after dinner and went to bed at eleven o'clock. She slept uninterrupted until seven o'clock the next morning. She nearly missed the early morning walk through the vineyards with the horses that she was so keen on. Elsa had explained that she loves walking. She regrets not having enough opportunity to do much walking where she lives. After the mindfulness session that morning, I sat down with Elsa to do the VAK test and discuss the various meditation techniques. I wanted to help her choose one that she would find easy to incorporate into her daily life. She was a kinesthetic learner and not altogether surprisingly, she opted for walking meditation. I was glad that she did. Walking meditation would be the perfect meditation method for Elsa.

She wanted to know more about walking meditation. I explained that walking meditation is basically mindful walking. "But is walking meditation real meditation? she wanted to know. I shared Chandresh Bhardwaj, founder of the Break The Norms meditation program's words with her: "It's a myth that meditation happens only when you light candles or incense and sit cross-legged." Instead, he explains, "When you are deeply involved in any activity, you become meditative."

Elsa's Meditation Method: Walking Meditation
1. What is Walking Meditation?
2. How does Walking Meditation work?
3. Enriching Walking Meditation: Combination with other methods

I decided to explain further using a practical example. One of our Friesian mares, Aurore, was peacefully munching away, not two metres from where we were sitting. When Aurore (Rosie to her closest friends) was a foal, we spent a lot of time introducing her to the world. We wanted her to grow up to be a confident and contented adult horse. One of the ways we did this, was to take her for long walks through the countryside.

Now Rosie was never going to be an easy-to-intimidate horse. She is insatiably curious about every new thing she comes across, but she is not stupid. She always carefully inspects a new discovery before she decides whether it is threatening to her in any way, or not.

Rosie's curious-but-cautious approach to life made walking along a country path with her an exercise in mindfulness. A hundred paces might take her thirty or more minutes. She had to inspect every grass poll and every blade of grass in every grass poll. She would sniff it and if it smelled appetising, she would take a bite. If it tasted good, she would eat it. We had to stop so that she could look closely at every butterfly fluttering by, at every bee gathering pollen in a flower, at every bird building a nest in a tree...and then we had to pause so that she could reflect on each of these new experiences. We certainly were going nowhere fast. When tractors came by, the driver had to stop so that she could inspect his machine - especially if the tractor had a piece of equipment attached that Rosie did not recognise. (Which was quite interesting to me too, I always wonder what all the different bits and pieces are for.)

The reason I mentioned Rosie's intrepid forays into the French countryside is because it with Rosie that I first started to meditate while I walk. Never having enough minutes in the day, I thought that I might as well see if I can use our time together more effectively. I decided to combine the walk with a bit of meditation. I soon found out that it is not only possible to walk and meditate at the same time, but that walking meditation is a widely practised meditation technique. I found a lot of information online about how to do walking meditation.

Many people find sitting still in the same position for extended periods of time difficult. It may be because they find it difficult to concentrate while sitting still. I am thinking specifically about kinesthetic learners – people who can only learn if they can move at the same time. As school children, they would have been constantly scolded for fidgeting. I am also thinking of people with a physical condition, like arthritis, that makes sitting still painful.

For these people, walking meditation is an ideal solution. Walking meditation benefits both the body and the mind. Most meditation methods do, but here you have the added benefit of slow and sustained movement. This improves blood circulation and increases muscle and joint mobilisation. Some people also say that they find it easier to be aware of what is going on in their bodies while they are walking, than while they are sitting still.

Concentrating on your body while walking can also make you aware of your posture. This awareness may inspire you to walk with better posture and less tension, even when you are not meditating.

1. What exactly is walking meditation?

Jack Kornfield writes in his book "The Wise Heart," that walking meditation is a simple practice that develops calmness, connectedness, and embodied awareness. It can be done before or after sitting meditation or at any time on its own. The aim of walking meditation is to use the natural movement of walking to cultivate mindfulness.

Walking Meditation is Mindfulness Meditation in motion.

During walking meditation, the idea is to focus on the physical experience of walking. This will help you develop greater awareness of yourself and your surroundings without allowing yourself to be distracted by your thoughts. During our mindfulness and meditation workshops, we encourage our guests to try walking meditation by walking up and down the vineyards surrounding the farm. This allows our guests to enjoy walking outside without having to concentrate on the path itself. We also invite our guests to do walking meditation with the horses, following in Aurore's footsteps. We encourage our guests to pay particular attention to how fully aware the horses are of their own bodies and at the same time of their environment.

2. How does Walking Meditation work?

It still was not quite clear to Elsa how exactly one does walking meditation. It is really is very simple. I explained, "You switch off your computer. You put your phone on standby, pull on some comfortable walking shoes and you start walking. Outside, if you can. Personally, I love walking barefoot outside. It makes me feel properly grounded, but with our horses being such enthusiastically fertilisers, this is not always such a good idea!

You can do walking meditation almost anywhere. You can walk up and down a corridor or up and down a flight of stairs. You can even do it on a treadmill*. The choice is yours. I find it easier to walk where there are fewer people to bump into. It is one of the main reasons many of our guests come to the south of France – fewer people, less noise, less traffic, less stress, less pollution and less distraction. If it sounds too good to be true, visit Gascony: God's own Country on Pinterest (Margaretha's Muse) and see for yourself. We also have a lot of fresh air here. This is good for your lungs, enabling them to thoroughly oxygenate your moving muscles. We also have fresh water from our springs. Drinking some water before you start is a good idea. So is taking some water with you on your walk."

Usually, we encourage our guests to do a couple of walking meditations on their own, before they join us for a walking meditation with the horses. Elsa agreed to my suggestion, so I advised her that the way to start a walking meditation is by standing still and taking a few deep breaths. I went on, "It can be useful to take a few moments and focus on what you are going to do. A simple phrase like "Now I am going to do a five-minute walking meditation" will work well. Then you start walking at a relaxed, fairly slow but normal pace." I added, "You will find your attention drawn to the sights, smells and sounds around you as you walk. This is perfectly normal, just continually keep re-focusing on the physical sensation of walking. Notice your breathing. Count the number of steps you take while you are breathing in. Count the number you take while breathing out. You may notice that, as you walk, the number of the steps you take during each breath increases or decreases. Pay attention to the sensations in your body as you walk. Notice that your entire body is involved in the act of walking. Become aware of each of your feet individually. Notice the moment you place your heel on the ground. Notice the moment you transfer your weight to the ball of your foot and then to the tips of your toes. Register the feeling of lifting your foot off the ground and moving it forward.

Walking mindfully has six components: raising, lifting, pushing, dropping, touching, and pressing your foot on the ground. With practice, you will be able to feel each sensation separately. Notice the sensations in other parts of your body as you walk – your ankles, shins, calves, knees, thighs, hips, pelvis, back, chest, shoulders, arms, neck and head. If there is tension in any part of your body, make a conscious effort to let it go. At the end of your walking meditation, come to a natural stop. Spend a moment feeling grateful that you CAN walk, that you have clothes and shoes to walk in and that you have somewhere safe to walk.

When we are walking and meditating, we sometimes find ourselves distracted by something we see or hear. When this happens, all we have to do is to simply bring our attention back to the sensation of walking. If you absolutely have to look at something, it is best to acknowledge this impulse and to stop walking. Look at what you want to look at, listen to it, smell it or touch it, and then continue walking, concentrating on the movement."

I also pointed out to Elsa that it is worthwhile to remember that walking meditation is not about arriving at a certain destination. She should not do walking meditation with the intention of going anywhere specific. Even so, it is possible to do walking meditation on the way to somewhere. Her attention will then be, temporarily, focused on the process of walking and not on her destination. She might even decide to walk in one direction for a couple of minutes and then walk back the way she came. She could repeat this the whole time she does this meditation. Or she could simply walk in a circle. She could also use a Walking Meditation App to learn how to do walking meditation and track her progress.

3. Combining Walking Meditation with other Meditation Methods

Walking meditation can be combined with other meditation methods. I would like to mention three of them here:
- The Loving-Kindness Walking Meditation
- The Labyrinth Walking Meditation
- Taking a Poem for a Walk Meditation
- Stepping up the pace: Running Meditation

- The Loving-Kindness Walking Meditation

Loving-kindness meditation combines effortlessly with walking meditation (as it does with a writing meditation.) It basically involves spreading goodwill, to yourself and to others, by repeating the following phrases:

May I be filled with loving-kindness.
May I be safe from all danger.
May I be healthy in body and in mind.

May I be free from undue stress.
May I be happy.

I usually combine these phrases with my breathing. As I breathe in, I would say to myself, "May I be filled..." and as I breathe out, "...with loving kindness." The next step would be to focus on another person, someone you love:

May you be filled with loving-kindness.
May you be safe from all danger.
May you be healthy in body and mind.
May you be free from undue stress.
May you be happy.

From here, one could move on to friends, family, colleagues, community and church leaders. If you want to make this loving-kindness walking meditation especially meaningful, you could include not only people you like but also people you dislike. A study led by Barbara Fredrickson and published in the Journal of Personality and Social Psychology revealed that "the practice of loving-kindness meditations led to shifts in people's daily experiences of a wide range of positive emotions, including love, joy, gratitude, contentment, hope, pride, interest, amusement, and awe...They enabled people to become more satisfied with their lives and to experience fewer symptoms of depression."

- The Labyrinth Walking Meditation

I found a good definition of a meditation labyrinth at Wikipedia: "A labyrinth is an ancient symbol that relates to wholeness. It combines the imagery of the circle and the spiral on a meandering but purposeful path. A labyrinth represents a journey to our own centre and back again out into the world. Labyrinths have long been used as facilitators for meditation." One of the earliest labyrinths were found in Greece.

It dates back to 2500-2000 B.C. This labyrinth is called the Cretan labyrinth or the classic seven-circuit labyrinth. It consists of seven concentric circles. Christian labyrinths date back to 4th century. The Chartres labyrinth, laid into the cathedral floor at Chartres Cathedral, in France, dates from the thirteenth century. The Chartres design is a characteristic eleven-circuit labyrinth. It has eleven concentric circles.

It is true that when we are troubled by disturbing emotions or by unfortunate events, walking a labyrinth can help us resolve our inner conflict. It can still our minds. It can help us find possible solutions and alternative options. When we moved here, we decided that we would like to create our own labyrinth. We figured it could not be all that difficult to create a meditation labyrinth. Surely, all you need is a field with long grass and a lawnmower?

We have since gone off the idea, you will find out why as you read on.

A meditation labyrinth is not a maze, so no need to incorporate dead ends and hidden passageways. A meditation labyrinth consists of a single path that winds its way into the centre of the labyrinth. The person walking it follows the same path on their way to the centre of the labyrinth as on their way out. Perfectly simple. Or so we thought.

One walks a meditation labyrinth in 3 stages:

The first stage, at the entrance to the labyrinth, is when you ground yourself. This is the time to release tension. You consciously decide to leave all fears and worries at the entrance to the labyrinth. Here you focus on the problem you want to solve. You then follow the path, concentrating on walking mindfully, to the centre of the labyrinth.

The second stage is about finding, at the centre of the labyrinth, a solution to the problem you are trying to solve. You then return the same way you came to the labyrinth exit. Some people choose to spend time in the centre of the labyrinth, sitting quietly. Some do a writing meditation.

The third stage is about taking back into the world the solution to the problem you have discovered.

"Your life is a sacred journey. It is about change, growth, discovery, movement, transformation, continuously expanding your vision of what is possible, stretching your soul, learning to see clearly and deeply, listening to your intuition, taking courageous challenges at every step along the way. You are on the path... exactly where you are meant to be right now... And from here, you can only go forward, shaping your life story into a magnificent tale of triumph, of healing of courage, of beauty, of wisdom, of power, of dignity, and of love." Caroline Adams

A meditation labyrinth is symbolic of the path that we are on, each and every one of us, during our lifetime. It symbolises our life's journey to the centre of our inner self and out again with a better understanding of who we are.

By now, you may be wondering what was so difficult about creating a meditation labyrinth. We had a field, we had long grass and we had a lawnmower. Well, it was like this. The field, the only one large enough, was not flat. It had a slope. There were wetter and dryer patches, smoother and stonier patches and several rather deep holes. The grass was too long and too wet and the lawnmower was set too low. We chose a ground plan that was too ambitious and too complicated. We didn't get the layout right, which meant we cut grass that should have been left long – not an easy-to-repair mistake. We did rather enjoy ourselves, messing about, and we did have a good laugh at ourselves. Eventually, we gave up, cut the whole field with the tractor, levelled it and filled up the holes.

Three weeks later, we had another go. The grass grows so fast here in the spring you can just about hear it growing. This time, we chose a simple and straightforward plan. The grass was dry. The repaired lawn mower was set to high. We soon had a respectable meditation labyrinth in our backyard, right between the raised vegetable beds and the wildflower field.

Our most impressive labyrinth lasted exactly 3 days. On the third day after its creation, the horses escaped from their paddock and ate their way happily round our precious labyrinth. We had to accept that some things are just not meant to be.

- Taking a Poem for a Walk Meditation

In the book, Wanderlust: A History of Walking, Rebecca Solnit says: "Walking, ideally, is a state in which the mind, the body, and the world are aligned, as though they were three characters finally in conversation together, three notes suddenly making a chord. Walking allows us to be in our bodies and in the world without being made busy by them. It leaves us free to think without being wholly lost in our thoughts."

There are many suitable poems that can be read or recited during a "Take a poem for a walk" meditation. One poem may resonate with someone and do next to nothing for another. I often recommend "Walk Slowly," a poem written by Danna Faulds, to our guests. Choosing a poem with a rhythm that combines well with one's breathing rhythm works best.

"Walking is magic. Can't recommend it highly enough. I read that Plato and Aristotle did much of their brilliant thinking together while ambulating. The movement, the meditation, the health of the blood pumping, and the rhythm of footsteps... this is a primal way to connect with one's deeper self." – Paula Cole

Walking meditation, as a meditation method, suited Elsa perfectly. She found that she could easily incorporate a ten-minute walking meditation on her way to work. She also often did a walking meditation on the way back home. This helped her to leave the office stress behind and to focus her attention on enjoying the evening with her boys. When she came back a year later for another workshop, she was much calmer and she looked much happier.

– Stepping up the pace: Running Meditation

There is another method of movement meditation that I would like to mention here, because I practice it. Not in detail, because unlike walking meditation that nearly everyone can do, running is more of an acquired taste. I run just about every day because as Dr. George Sheehan says, "I run each day to preserve the self I attained the day before. And coupled with this is the desire to secure the self yet to be. There can be no let-up. If I do not run, I will eventually lose all I have gained–and my future with it."

I have been running regularly these past 30 years. I started long before I knew what meditation was. What I did know, was that running made me feel less stressed. After a run, I felt calmer, more centred, more in control. I solved many of life's problems while running. I wrote many blog posts, articles and book chapters while running. Running is essential to both my physical and my mental well-being, so much so that when I could no longer see well enough to run outside, I started running on a treadmill. These days, often while watching a video of running horses, but that is another story I will come to later.

A study in Medicine and Science in Sports and Exercise revealed that even 30 minutes of running time on a treadmill could instantly lift someone's mood. I am living proof of this effect. Several books have been written about using running as a promoter for self-growth, from Haruki Murakami's What I Talk About When I Talk About Running to Jen A. Miller's Running: A Love Story to Caleb Daniloff's Running Ransom Road. Running combined with meditation can potentially make both our bodies and our minds stronger. A 2016 study published in Translational Psychiatry found that combining meditation with running (or walking!) reduced symptoms of depression by 40% for depressed participants.

I am not trying to convince you to take up either running. If you do decide to give it a go though, remember that one should never take up any demanding physical activity without seeing one's doctor for a full check-up. Trust me. If you are already a runner, and you want to add mindfulness meditation to your long, slow runs, I suggest you practice on a treadmill first while watching a guided running meditation on YouTube or you can use an app like Lucid.

Equine-facilitated Mindfulness Meditation: Mastering Walking Meditation with Horses

Walking meditation, especially with the horses, is a practical way to cultivate mindfulness, that is why I incorporated it into our mindfulness and meditation workshops.

The horse that taught me most about walking meditation was called Aurileo, or Leo, for short, because he had the courageous heart of a lion. He was a rescue horse from Portugal, a golden palomino who must have had many admirers when he was still working in the bull-fighting arena. We assumed that he was sent to the butcher's, from where we rescued him because he lost his nerve after being gored through the neck by a bull.

When he came to us, he was terrified of people, especially of men. In the four happy years he was with us, he regained not only his trust in people, but also his self-confidence and his self-respect. It took nearly a year before he was approachable. Once he was willing to walk on a lead, we set off across the meadows, through the orchards, along the vineyards, around the lakes and into the forests of this breathtakingly beautiful region. Sometimes we walked slowly, sometimes we walked fast, sometimes we stopped to admire an awe-inspiring view.

Every second of our walk we were acutely aware of each other and of our surroundings. I had to be 100% present in each moment because he was liable to bolt at the slightest unfamiliar sight or sound. I also had to remain thoroughly calm, because he was intensely aware of my mental state. The moment he thought I saw or heard something worrying, he became a nervous wreck. Distancing myself from my thoughts, observing them without interacting with them produced a profound sense of well-being in Leo. It was, initially, the only way I could communicate with him, the only way I could calm him.

Leo sadly died of colic after he had been with us for four years, but for those 4 years, he was unconditionally loved by everyone who knew him. Leo also taught me quite a lot about myself and about equine-assisted personal development.

Could walking meditation be something for you? Could you design your own unique way of walking while meditating, a way of meditating that can work for you, while remembering that this journey is uniquely yours, no one else's. The path has to be your own. You cannot imitate somebody else's journey and still be true to yourself. Are you prepared to honour your uniqueness in this way?" Jon Kabat-Zinn

The next chapter is about Working Meditation: the perfect way to incorporate meditation into an already bursting-at-the-seams daily routine, without having to sacrifice a single precious minute of your busy day.

*Doing a walking meditation on a treadmill may sound like a boring idea. It is, however, very useful for people who are visually handicapped. It also makes life easier when you first start practising walking meditation, allowing you to concentrate on the sensation of walking without having to worry about where you are putting your feet. It is also convenient when the weather is unsuitable. I not only love walking meditation. I am also a fan of running meditation. I sometimes even do my walking or running meditation on a treadmill.

Chapter 6

Working Meditation

Axelle's Letter

"Dear Margaretha

Yesterday, while looking for information online about mindfulness, I found your website. You answered several of the most pressing questions I had about being mindful. I have to decide whether it will be worthwhile to allocate part of my day to mindfulness. I am specifically interested in mindfulness meditation. I also read a few of your blog posts and here and there I had to laugh out loud, especially this one: Going on a retreat? Don't forget your fur coat, diamonds and high heels. The laughing did me a lot of good. I have not had an opportunity to laugh like that in a long time.

I have never meditated before. I am a meditation virgin. I am interested in finding out how to meditate because my doctor has suggested that it may be good for my health. I feel a bit intimidated, I have to admit. I am not sure if it is something that I would be able to do and keep on doing. I cannot imagine sitting still for any period of time thinking about nothing much. I feel it would be a waste of time. Time is very precious to me. However, I do need to do something about my health, and I need to do this as soon as possible. I have recently been diagnosed with a stomach ulcer. My doctor says it is stress related. He is probably right. I have started taking medication, but so far, the medication has not been of much use. My doctor says this is not surprising since I have done nothing to deal with my ever-rising stress levels.

If I am going to start meditating, I am going to need some help, that is why I am interested in your workshops. I need proper instruction. Learning how to be more mindful and how to meditate in the presence of other people with the same goal appeals to me. So does escaping to the countryside for a few days. I shall not be able to get away for the full seven days. I wish I could! I would like to attend for five days, during the September workshop, if that is possible.

On your site, you ask that applicants write a bit about why they want to attend your workshops. As I have mentioned, I urgently need help with stress management. I am a boulangère (baker) in a busy little town near Paris. I also make and sell patisserie (cakes) in my bakery. I get up at three o'clock every morning. I arrive at the boulangerie at four o'clock. I immediately start preparing the day's bread. I still do much of the work myself, although I do have a couple of machines to make life easier. I open the shop at six. I work until six o'clock in the evening. I do take a day off every week. I only work half-day on Sundays, but I am usually so exhausted that I spend most of my time off sleeping. From time to time I manage to get some help in the shop. As you probably know, it is very difficult these days to interest young people in working long hours, even for decent pay.

I took the boulangerie over five years ago, from my aunt. She left it to me in her will. At the time, it was floundering. My aunt had lost interest and did not do much to expand or even retain her current customers. The shop was on the verge of bankruptcy. I spent the first three years building up the business. I paid off the debts I had inherited. It was a difficult time. Luckily, I have a very understanding bank manager! From the fourth year, the business started to show a small profit, and this year it is starting to look healthy. Sadly, I am not! The prolonged and constant stress is destroying my health. And my sanity, for that matter.

This is why I find meditation difficult. I cannot imagine sitting still for any amount of time without thinking about the shop. Sitting still would mean wasting time, time that I could have spent working. Mindfulness is a difficult concept for me too. Even when I am working, I am frantically multi-tasking, trying to get everything done that needs doing.

I am not married. I do not have time for a relationship. I am starting to miss that. I would like to share my life with someone. I just do not know where I will find the time to invest in a relationship. Maybe if I can find a way to manage my stress better, I could also find a way to manage my time better.

My brothers and I grew up on a farm, so I am quite familiar with horses. Even so, I am amazed to find out that horses are now helping people with psychological problems! I am very interested in this. I definitely want to learn more about equine-assisted personal development and mindfulness meditation, especially since I read your "What is Equine-assisted Experiential Learning?" page last night.

I have subscribed to your blog. I have also bought your book "You ARE good enough." All this worrying is eroding my self-confidence. Now I just need to find time to read it!

If you could let me know if you can fit me in that week, I would be very grateful. I close the shop for two weeks in September every year, so coming at that time will suit me well.

Kind Regards

Axelle."

Assessing Axelle's problem

Axelle came to our September workshop that year. She was a lively brunette, bursting with energy and a joie de vivre that the stress she suffered from had not quite managed to extinguish. Soon after her arrival, she offered to bake the bread while she stayed with us. Initially, my impulse was to decline. I thought it would be better if she used her time with us to relax and recharge her batteries. When I had time to think it over, I changed my mind. I suspected that Axelle would not be able to sit still and meditate quietly. Not at this point in her life. As for being mindful, she has fallen into the habit of multi-tasking, a difficult habit to unlearn in five days. We were going to have to work with what we have, working being the operative word.

I gratefully accepted her offer. I insisted that I was only doing so under the provision that she uses this time to practice mindful working meditation. She looked at me in astonishment. "Working Meditation? What is working meditation?"

Axelle's Meditation Method: Working Meditation

Not surprisingly, Axelle's VAK test revealed that she is a kinesthetic learner with a strong gustatory component. Chances were good that mindful working meditation would suit Axelle, especially as she could practise it while she was working. We talked about working meditation and its possibilities by addressing Axelle's questions:

1. What is working meditation?
2. What are the benefits of Working Meditation?
3. How can I implement Working Meditation?

1. What is working meditation?

Here on the farm, we offer our workshop participants the opportunity to engage in mindful working meditation. Working meditation, like walking meditation and writing meditation, is mindfulness meditation in action. During mindful working meditation, the point is not to rush through the task so that you can have more time for meditation, but rather to use it as an opportunity to practice mindfulness in action. It is a time to observe and let go of the many attitudes, beliefs, and feelings that interfere with having a meaningful awareness of the task at hand, no matter what that task might be. It has the additional benefit of a meditation practice that can be seamlessly incorporated into our daily lives.

On a day-to-day basis, we spend a lot of time working: not only while we are at work, but also while we are at home. We prepare meals. We clean the house. We mow the lawn. We wash, iron and fold the laundry. Each of these activities can be done mindfully, thus enriching the experience and making it more worthwhile. I introduced Axelle to working meditation because it is a meditation method that she could do while she was working, thus bypassing her worry about "wasting time doing nothing." This could even fit in with her addiction to multi-tasking. She would be working and mindfully meditating at the same time. Axelle and I needed a serious talk about multi-tasking before she left. There is nothing wrong with multi-tasking, as long as it is balanced by mindfulness.

Working meditation is one of the most useful methods of meditation to learn. We all have to work. The idea is to pay attention to each movement – however small – that you make while doing the work required of you. This will help you master the art of being fully present in the moment. By training ourselves to pay attention moment by moment to where we are and what we are doing, mindfulness helps us to realise that between stimulus and response there is the opportunity to choose a reaction. Mindfulness enables us to function better in a high-performance environment. In the workplace, this can lead to higher productivity, better teamwork, increased creativity, accurate communication and quick resolution of conflict. Mindfulness expert Mirabai Bush, famous for introducing the Google workforce to mindfulness, says: "Over time with mindfulness, we learn to develop the inner resources that will help us navigate through difficult, trying, and stressful situations with more ease, comfort and grace.

I explained that just like sitting meditation, working meditation means repeatedly bringing our attention back to the present moment. Just as the mind will wander off in thought during sitting meditation so it can also wander while we are working. I reassured her that noticing a distracting thought surfacing is perfectly normal. It happens to all of us. The trick is to acknowledge the thought without giving any attention to it and to then let it fade away again. Axelle practised the technique in the five days she was with us. While she was discussing working meditation with the other participants, one of them suggested that she may even be able to use this technique to grow her business. The suggestion was that she makes a single "hand-made with love" batch of bread per day and market this as her boulangerie's speciality. The idea was that she repeats a loving-kindness script to herself while she is making the bread. As far as I know, she is still doing this, the concept is a huge success with her customers.

Equine-facilitated Mindfulness Meditation

Our horses love the working meditation activity. Luckily, many guests choose to groom one of the horses as the "work" they want to do. Grooming benefits both the horse and the person who does the grooming. The horse mainly physically and the person who does the grooming both physically - it is very good exercise! - as well as mentally. Grooming can be a limitlessly enriching experience. I suspect the main reason for this is because it involves our sense of touch.

It seems to me that people touch each other less and less. When I was a young doctor, doctors hugged their patients when they felt the patient needed a hug. These days, patients and doctors do not hug each other anymore. It is seen as highly inappropriate. It is not only in consultation rooms that hugging has become a taboo. Dr Tiffany Field, head of the Touch Research Institute at the University of Miami's Miller School of Medicine, conducted a study to find out how often people touch each other in public places. She found that nobody was touching each other anymore. Everyone had their smartphones in their hands. "I think social media has been really detrimental to touch," Dr Field said. "Being on your phone is distancing people physically from each other. It used to be in airports, you'd see people hugging and napping on each other. Now they're just not touching."

In our technology-saturated world, neutral, non-sexual human touch is in danger of becoming obsolete. Despite the benefits of modern technology, it remains vital for us to touch each other regularly in order to thrive.

Why? Because comforting physical contact, as experienced when we hug, decreases disease incidence and strengthens our immune systems. A study conducted by the Carnegie Mellon University (CMU) has revealed that hugs can, in fact, help fight off infections. The study, led by Sheldon Cohen, who is a Professor of Psychology at CMU's Dietrich College of Humanities and Social Sciences, was published in the Psychological Science journal. It also found that people who had greater social support and experienced more hugs were more protected from stress and stress-related infections.

What is more, touching can increase understanding and trust between individuals. Touch helps people bond. Daniel Keltner, the founding director of the Greater Good Science Centre and Professor of Psychology at University of California, Berkeley, cites the work of neuroscientist

Edmund Ross, who found that physical touch activates the brain's orbito-frontal cortex, the seat of kindness and compassion. According to Keltner, "Touch signals safety and trust; it soothes. Touch calms cardiovascular stress. It activates the body's vagus nerve, which is intimately involved with our compassionate response."

Touch can also help people and horses bond. We have a beautiful Friesian mare here called Tess des Sources Sacrées. She came to us because her owner found her impossible, if not downright dangerous, to handle. When she first arrived, we decided to give as long as she needs to settle in before we ask her to do anything. All I did, once or twice a week, was to groom her, from head to hoof. Initially, she did not much appreciate my efforts. She did not know me, she did not trust me and I had no business touching her vulnerable underbelly. What eventually swung the balance in my favour was the annoying itch she had in both her ears. She discovered that I did have a use after all. From then onward, each grooming session started with a good scratch. Inside her ears, behind her ears, down her neck, along her sides and back to the irritating little spot on her croup that she cannot reach herself. By the time I got to her croup, Tess was thoroughly relaxed and could surrender without inhibitions to the soothing effect of the grooming brush.

During the workshop, Axelle did a fair amount of horse grooming, also in her time off, explaining that she had forgotten how soul-soothing an experience it can be.

2. Working Meditation Benefits

Working meditation allows our guests to reconnect with their environment, with nature and with each other. A large percentage of today's workforce spend their working lives in offices. Working outside in the fresh air and natural light is often a deeply satisfying experience for them. When combined with formal meditation, working in the garden, by the lake or on the land can become a symbolic act of giving and receiving, of nourishing and being nourished.

A working meditation session here on the farm can also be a learning experience for our guests. We aim to be as self-sufficient as possible – always with an eye on sustainability and leaving as light a footprint as possible. Our vegetable garden is organic. We use companion planting to control pests and diseases and permaculture to make the best use of water and organic waste. We have a beehive for honey. The bees also fertilise the fruit trees in our orchard. We use the horses' manure as compost for the vegetable garden, orchard, flower garden and paddocks. Working meditation participants can discover a variety of eco-friendly practices while working here mindfully.

In general, working meditation can also increase our attention span, make us physically fitter, increase our stamina and resilience, add to our problem-solving skills and enable us to sleep better.

3. Implementing Working Meditation

We introduce all our workshop participants to working meditation, to demonstrate how they can incorporate meditation into their daily lives. This is especially useful on days when they might not have time for formal sitting meditation practice. There is always work that needs doing on a farm like ours. It may involve gathering fallen leaves, weeding the kitchen garden or turning over the compost heap. Our guests choose the type of work they want to do. We adjust the work according to our guests' abilities. As with all our activities, full instructions are given beforehand so that our guests can get the maximum benefit. I explained to Axelle, that instead of thinking of a hundred other things while she is gathering the ingredients, mixing the dough, kneading it and then putting it into the oven, she should focus one hundred per cent of her attention on each individual task. She should use all five her senses to enrich the experience. She should notice how the spoon feels in her hand: hot or cold, smooth or uneven, heavy or light. She should use her sense of smell to determine each ingredient's individual aroma. She should use her sense of hearing to identify the various little sounds that accompany the bread making process: The sound of the spoon against the bowl when she is stirring, the sound of the oven door opening and closing, the sound of the oven's fan in the background. She should use her sight to marvel at the different shades and changing colours at she mixes in the ingredients. She should do the kneading with her hands instead of using a machine, when she has time. She laughed when I suggested this, explaining that she often kneads the dough to get rid of her frustrations...

Axelle could see how mindfulness can help her manage her business more effectively and how meditation could help her cope better with stress. She developed additional coping strategies while taking part in personal development activities with the horses. She practised stopping to assess a situation mindfully, instead of reacting impulsively. She felt more in control of her destiny. Her health gradually improved.

Mindfulness, as practised during mindful working meditation, will help you to:

- focus intently,
- be more aware of yourself and your environment,
- listen more carefully,
- understand better,
- communicate clearly and
- concentrate effortlessly.

It is clear that working mindfully here in the south of France will not just provide the immediate benefit of doing physical exercise outside in the fresh air, but it can also be useful to participants when they return to their workplace where they can incorporate what they have practised during the workshop into their daily work and home lives. If you would like to find out more about our mindfulness meditation workshops, please visit us at our website EquineGuidedGrowth.com

In the next chapter, we are coming to another of my favourite meditation methods, music meditation!

Chapter 7

Music Meditation

Before you read this chapter's letter, I would like you to take part in an experiment. I would like you to experience the following music video on YouTube: Albannach - Edinburgh Festival Fringe or if you prefer the soundtrack only: Albannach - Albacadabra and answer this question: Is there something about drums or is it just me? Replies to margarethamontagu@gmail.com

Sarah's Letter

"Dear Margaretha,

I don't know if you will remember me. I was a patient of yours when we were both living and working in Oxford. We actually met at choir practice. I was one of the altos. Can you believe that it is more than fifteen years since we last saw each other? I chanced upon your website while looking for more information about mindfulness. I thought, hey, I know this lady. I see you go by your married name now. As your books are still published under your maiden name, I recognised you. Delighted to have found you again.

I am still married to the same chap, but we are having a few problems. I have read somewhere that mindfulness can help strengthen relation-ships. This relationship certainly needs strengthening. We are not at loggerheads or anything, we have just drifted apart somewhat. I think Andrew only started singing in the choir after you had left, so you would not have met him. Let me tell you more about our problems, then you can let me know if mindfulness might help us. I read that researchers have proved scientifically that mindfulness can help couples, so I have got high hopes!

Andrew and I have been married for thirty years. We have lived in Oxford for all our married life. I grew up in Iffley. Andrew originally comes from Scotland. He is a lecturer at one of the colleges. We are by no means wealthy, but we are fairly comfortable. The children are doing reasonably well. The oldest two have started to work. The two younger ones are still studying. All have chosen careers that should enable them to make their way in the world. Assuming that is going to be possible. Not easy for young people to get onto the property ladder these days. Three of the four are currently in relationships. We like our prospective son- and daughters-in-law and we are looking forward to grandchildren one day.

The mortgage on our house in Headington has been paid off. We have a little bit of extra money to spend on our hobbies. We enjoy travelling. I have always been into music. Andrew slightly less so, but he does enjoy singing in the choir. We are both very keen on classical music. We try to attend as many concerts as we can. Living in Oxford, we have had the opportunity to attend many excellent concerts these last thirty years!

All four of our children have flown the nest now. We have the typical empty nest set-up. Since the last one has left, Andrew and I only have each other for company. I think we have both noticed that our relationship is not as healthy as it can be. We do not seem to have that much to say to each other anymore. We have both changed in the last thirty years. We no longer know each other all that well. The children bound us together, but now that they are gone... I am willing to work at our relationship and I think Andrew is too. Andrew does not want to see a marriage counsellor. He says that surely our relationship is not in such bad shape. I am not so sure. I think I could convince him to spend a week in the south of France, though, if you think that would be helpful.

We both love France. A few years ago, we even thought about buying a holiday home somewhere in the south. We have spent many happy holidays in different parts of France while the children were growing up. If Andrew and I can resurrect our relationship, I think we might both want to realise this dream. We might even want to retire to France, in a few years. We used to be able to discuss everything when we were younger. Now it is much more difficult to talk.

There is nothing seriously wrong with our relationship. It has just become a bit stale. We might be a bit more impatient with each other. We are less tolerant of each other's faults, now that we have the house to ourselves. Maybe we have just run out of things to say to each other. For so many years, we mostly talked to each other about the children. We talked about the children's needs, their problems, their achievements, their highs and their lows. Now we can't seem to find anything to say to each other. I am also going through the final stages of the menopause, which is not helping. I suspect Andrew is getting fed up with this. I have had symptoms for a good five years so far. We do have some good times together, but these are becoming less and less frequent now. In a way, we are both trying to work out who we are now that the children have left.

There has been some talk at Andrew's work about laying people off. At his age, it would be difficult to find another job. He is still much too young to retire. Our savings could tide us over should he lose his job, but not indefinitely. I am working part-time as a secretary at a local law firm, but this does not bring in an awful lot. We have been quite stressed lately. Since we find it difficult to communicate, the tension has also become part of our relationship.

At the moment, I am looking at your mindfulness meditation workshop the last week in August. Could you let me know if this would be possible? Assuming you think that mindfulness could help us. I do not think Andrew will be interested in attending the workshop itself. He might be interested in doing some wine tasting. I saw on your website that non-participating partners are also welcome. Could you let me know more about that?

Neither of us knows anything much about meditation. Or about horses! In all honesty, Andrew finds it all a bit too airy-fairy to be of much use.

Looking forward to hearing from you
  Sarah Blake."

I did remember Sarah. It would have been difficult not too. She was a lively redhead, always full of energy, always bustling about. She was one of the best altos in the choir. She was always smiling when I knew her or she wasn't laughing out loud. I even remembered Andrew vaguely, a tall, thin and studious type. I must have seen him for a flu jab or something, once or twice. I was sorry to hear that they were having problems.

Assessing Sarah's problem

Not knowing how Andrew felt about all this, complicated matters somewhat. It has indeed been proven that mindfulness can be of use to couples. I e-mailed Sarah to let her know that she would be very welcome at the August workshop. Andrew would be equally welcome as a non-participating guest. Luckily, I still had a nice and spacious double room left, with a window to the east. Some spectacular sunrises are visible from this room. Sitting up in bed, sipping their early morning coffee or tea, they may find it easier to talk. The guest wing has its own kitchen. Our guests often make themselves an early morning cuppa, before they go for an early morning walk.

I decided to put her mind at rest about Andrew coming as a non-participating guest first. Many of our workshop participants have friends, partners and spouses who would love a trip to the sun-baked south of France but who do not want to attend a mindfulness meditation workshop. I reassured Sarah that Andrew would not feel excluded. Our aim is to enable everyone to escape the daily grind and enjoy their stay here. Some accompanying partners decide to attend one of our walking and wine tasting workshops, during their stay.

Non-participating guests share in everything the workshop offers except for the meditation and the mindfulness sessions. There is loads to do on the farm and in the immediate vicinity: walking, cycling, sightseeing, shopping, kayaking, water skiing, fishing, golfing, wine tasting or just relaxing. As soon as the participants leave for their meditation sessions, their partners can settle back and luxuriate in the peace and quiet. In bed. Here everyone can unwind. Our guests sleep deeply and soundly in the silent, star-filled night. They wake up refreshed and full of energy. Breathing the fresh, herb-scented air and drink pure spring water helps them to relax and rejuvenate body and soul.

During the day, non-participating guests can relax in a hammock in the woods, on a deck chair by the lake or on a blanket in the orchard. The more adventurous can spend the endless sun-drenched days exploring the unspoilt countryside, medieval fortified villages, bustling fruit and vegetable markets, brocantes and antique fairs, fascinating museums and art collections…We recommend hiring a car for the duration of the holiday to give non-participating guests the chance to explore the many historic sites, golf courses, spas, water parks, street markets and vineyards.

Andrew will be able to

1. visit the region's outstanding Armagnac, Madiran and Saint Mont vineyards
2. play golf at one or more of the excellent 18-hole golf courses in the vicinity
3. attend a bullfight or a course landaise or go skiing in the winter
4. luxuriate in the thermal spa at Bagnères-de-Bigorre, Cazaubon, Lectoure or Pau
5. attend a stage de pilotage at the motor racing circuit at Nogaro
6. walk, run or cycle through the pine woods of the Landes
7. practice a hobby like photography or painting
8. go swimming, canoeing and surfing on the Atlantic Coast
9. spend time shopping in the exquisite boutiques of Bordeaux, Pau, Tarbes, Toulouse, Agen and Mont de Marsan
10. attend the horse racing at the "English" city of Pau – home of the oldest golf course on the continent
11. walk a part of the St Jacques de Compostelle route towards Spain
12. discover the regional irresistible cuisine including foie gras, magret de canard, cassoulet and canard confit

Despite this not-exhaustive list of tempting activities, I wondered if I might be able to interest Andrew in music meditation. Sarah's VAK test revealed that she is a strong auditory learner. From Andrew's speech and expressions, I gathered that he may be an auditory interpreter too. Music is the one passion that they continue to share. Music meditation could be of great use to them. It will help them cope with the stress generated by Andrew's job insecurity. I suggested to Andrew that he was more than likely already practising a form of music meditation without realising. He gave me a doubtful look.

Sarah's Meditation Method: Music Meditation

Both Andrew and Sarah were keen to find out more. There are as many different types of meditation techniques as there are different types of people. I explained to Andrew and Sarah that according to Fleming's Visual Auditory Kinaesthetic (VAK) Learning model, most people possess a dominant or preferred learning style. They are both auditory learners and interpreters that is why music meditation may appeal specifically to them.

Auditory learners best learn through listening. I also pointed out that although the VAK learning model provides an easy and quick way to assess people's preferred learning styles and to design learning methods that match people's preferences, it is not fool proof.

I added that people who have predominantly auditory skills may find music as the focus of meditation especially beneficial. Auditory learners will probably find music as background to meditation unbearable distracting. Music works better for auditory learners when it is the focus of the meditation session. Music meditation can, however, also benefit visual learners, as well as kinesthetic learners. As long as the latter is allowed to move (dance!) during the session. Visual and kinesthetic learners who are stuck inside a building in the middle of a busy and noisy city can find background music a useful addition to meditation.

Andrew and Sarah had a few pertinent questions:
1. What is Music Meditation?
2. Can Mindful Music Meditation help us rebuild our relationship?
3. How does one meditate to music?
4. Can you meditate while making music?

1. What is Music Meditation?

There is a difference between listening to music and music meditation. There is also a difference between music meditation - music as the focus of meditation - and music as background to meditation. Most guided meditations on YouTube have some or other background soundtrack, be that music, nature or animal sounds. This works for some auditory interpreters but not for others. Music as a background to meditation can be a distraction if the listener does not like the type of music the recorder has chosen. It may be difficult to concentrate on your breathing if you keep getting distracted by the background music. If you have chosen music yourself and the music you are listening to is the focus of your meditation, the experience will be very different.

Many people believe relaxation is the primary goal of meditation. During meditation, they often choose to listen to relaxing music. There is nothing wrong with this. As such, meditation is an excellent stress management tool. Mindfulness meditation, now one of the most popular western meditation techniques, focuses on awareness. With mindfulness meditation, relaxation is not the main aim. Non-judgemental awareness and presence in-the-moment is. If you choose to listen to music as your meditation practice, your focus is solely on the music. If you want it to be a mindfulness meditation practice, you also allow yourself to become aware of what is happening inside you while you listen to the music. You're exploring your relationship with the music and your reaction to the music. You can listen to any music that you want to during a mindfulness music meditation. It might be soothing and relaxing or it might be stimulating and uplifting.

Music as meditation differs from other forms of meditation. Music makes a contribution to the meditation session. If you concentrate fully on the music you are mindfully listening to, the type of music you have chosen could have an emotional influence on you. Music is a language. It bypasses our conscious mind and speaks directly to our unconscious mind.

Happiness, anger, melancholy, joy, frustration, pain... All these can be communicated through music. The music that you are listening to with your heart, mind, body and soul can have a positive or negative effect on you. Researchers in an emerging discipline, Music Therapy, are beginning to document the psychological and physical effects of listening to music. Research suggests that the effects of listening to specific kinds of music can be fundamentally good for our bodies, minds and spirits. It is important to keep this in mind when you choose the music you want to listen to during a music meditation.

"Music expresses that which cannot be put into words and that which cannot remain silent." Victor Hugo

Andrew is a Scot, so I suggested they start by listening to some Scottish drums, like those you experienced at the beginning of this chapter. They were both immediately captivated, from the first drum beat. In fact, they reacted much the same as my horses sometimes do to the sound of rhythmic drum beats: they froze where they were and remained focused on the sound until the last beat.

Gary Diggins says, the Psychology Today, "We moderns are the last people on the planet to uncover what older cultures have known for thousands of years: The act of drumming contains a therapeutic potential to relax the tense, energise the tired, and soothe the emotionally wounded." Professor Michael Winkelman, in his study Complementary Therapy for Addiction: "Drumming Out Drugs" says, "Research reviews indicate that drumming enhances recovery through inducing relaxation and enhancing theta-wave production and brain-wave synchronisation. Drumming produces pleasurable experiences, enhanced awareness of preconscious dynamics, release of emotional trauma, and reintegration of self. Drumming alleviates self-centredness, isolation, and alienation, creating a sense of connectedness with self and others. Drumming provides a secular approach to accessing a higher power and applying spiritual perspectives." Quite a mouthful. In essence, as far as I can gather, it means drumming is good for us.

"Music can minister to minds diseased, pluck from the memory a rooted sorrow, raze out the written troubles of the brain, and with its sweet oblivious antidote, cleanse the full bosom of all perilous stuff that weighs upon the heart" William Shakespeare

Drums provide rhythm, and rhythm is the foundation of music.

As it happens, both my husband and I are musical. I sing in a choir or two. Both of us have regular lessons: my husband has piano lessons and I have singing lessons. Music is an essential part of our lives and our daily activities. Keeping this in mind, you will not be surprised to find out that we have a keyboard as well as a grand piano on the premises. We often invite our workshop guests to a choir concert or some or other musical recital...an ideal opportunity for them to practice mindful music meditation! During that week in August, the world-renowned annual Jazz in Marciac festival was taking place in a neighbouring village. Although we are not total Jazz fanatics, the atmosphere is usually so magical that we attend several times during the festival. It was the perfect opportunity to introduce both Sarah and Andrew to music meditation. My husband's piano teacher, Alain-Paul Gaillot, is a composer of classical music. His choir, Excelsis, was performing some of his latest compositions during that week. As Andrew and Sarah are fans of classical music, we decided to take them to this concert.

2. Mindful Music Meditation and Relationships

On the first day of Sarah's workshop, as usual, I explained to our workshop guests what mindfulness and meditation is and how it can benefit them. I might have emphasised ever so slightly how beneficial mindfulness can be to relationships. Although Andrew was not officially participating, he was lying in a hammock nearby reading a book, clearly with one ear on what I was saying.

A study evaluating the benefits of a mindfulness-based relationship enhancement program suggests that mindfulness enhances couples' satisfaction with their relationships, their closeness and their acceptance of each other, while reducing relationship stress. In fact, three months after participating in the study, couples were still experiencing these improvements.

I explained that mindfulness is a stress management and relationship enhancement skill that anyone can acquire and integrate into their lives. I pointed out that mindfulness offers us a method to calm ourselves when we feel anxious, frustrated, irritated or stressed. Mindfulness increases our awareness of what we are feeling. It gives us the opportunity to pause and decide how we want to react. It is easy to understand how this ability can lower our stress levels and improve our relationships.

Imagine, I said, that your partner says or does something that seriously annoys you. Instead of immediately launching a counter attack, you pause for a moment to acknowledge your anger. Having acknowledged your anger, you are able to distance yourself from it. You do not allow it to influence your decision about what to do next. This pause also gives you the chance to reflect on what your partner has said or done. You have time to make sure you are interpreting your partner's words or actions correctly. In this pause, you may even allow yourself to look at the situation from your partner's point of view. You might even understand why your partner is behaving the way he/she is. You might find yourself feeling compassionate towards your partner. You might be able to remind yourself of the positive characteristics of your relationship. You can choose to react in a way that will not be detrimental to your relationship. A way that is not based on unresolved issues from your past. Mindfulness helps you notice the impact that your behaviour has on your partner.

In her book, "Rewire your brain for love: Creating vibrant relationships using the science of mindfulness," Marsha Lucas says, "You still have your emotions. They just don't hijack you." Mindfulness helps us to make choices in the heat of the moment that can serve instead of destroy our relationship. "The heat of the moment isn't a great time for your brain to remember all of those helpful hints you've read. You ideally want 'presence of mind' to be wired in and ready to roll at a millisecond's notice," Lucas said.

Mindfulness can also help us become more attentive listeners. Attentive listening is the key to all effective communication. Without the ability to listen effectively; messages are easily misunderstood. Communication quickly breaks down. Effective listening requires concentration. The problem is that most people do not listen with the intent to understand. They listen with the intent to reply. Not so long ago I wrote a blog post called Controversial Listening Skills that reflects my personal experience.

Having effective listening skills also means paying attention not only to what is being said but also to how it is being said. It means being aware of both verbal and non-verbal messages. What is more, mindfulness meditation is essentially about listening to yourself, to your body and to your mind. What greater compliment can you pay yourself than to listen to yourself with full attention?

I believe that helping people improve their ability to listen and so improve their communication skills also improves their relationships. We spend a fair amount of time on this subject during our mindfulness workshops. We use equine-assisted experiential learning (EEL) to help our workshop participants practice listening more attentively and communicate more effectively.

Horses are highly sensitive to what is NOT being said, in other words, to non-verbal communication. During an EEL session, our workshop participants learn that they need to communicate accurately, openly and honestly. They also learn to pay attention to our horses' body language as this is how our horses usually communicate. Participants thus quickly master advanced communication skills that can enhance their relationships.

Our most sympathetic equine listener is without any doubt the Duc d'Alegria. He is such a gentleman. He will stand there for hours, listening intently, as you share your innermost fears and hopes with him. He will breathe slowly and deeply while he listens to you, especially if he thinks you are distressed, to help calm you and to make it easier for you to process your experience. He does the same with our other horses. He can often be seen, staring into the middle distance, with a clearly irritated mare by his side, swishing her tail while sharing her troubles.

"Of all the tools available to us in dealing with conflict, none is more important than attentive, intentional listening. Listening helps reduce resistance and opens our thinking to creative solutions. Listening not only clarifies the message but changes both the messenger and the listener. Listening makes it possible for both sides to have a change of heart. "Brian Muldoon

From the depths of his hammock, Andrew piped up, "So how does one actually do it?"

3. How to listen to Music as a Mindfulness Meditation

I replied, "Select a piece of music. You can choose any piece of music. If you are feeling stressed, I suggest a relaxing piece of music.

I recommend you use headphones, for two reasons. Firstly, because they effectively fill your head with music. Secondly, headphones can help to block out external sounds. This is useful if you are meditating somewhere noisy.

Before turning the music on, make sure you are comfortable. You can sit or lie down. I recommend the sun-loungers on the decking by the lake. Make sure you are neither hungry nor thirsty before you start. Take several long, slow, deep breaths to help yourself settle down and relax. Once you are relaxed, let your breath resume its natural rhythm.

Turn the music on and close your eyes. Focus on listening to the music. Allow the music to surround you, to fill you, to become part of you.

As you continue listening, occasionally ask yourself if you are still concentrating on the music. If your attention is drifting and you are distracted by other thoughts, merely notice that this is happening. Then bring your attention back to the music. You may need to bring your attention back to the music again and again. Do not worry about this. It is perfectly normal, it happens to everyone.

Once the music has finished, remain seated or lying down for a few more moments. Thank the musicians and composer for their efforts, quietly, to yourself.

Take a few minutes to think about the experience. Any strong emotions well up? Happiness, sadness, inspiration or irritation? Notice how music can influence your mood. As you know, music can make you feel relaxed, or music can make you feel energised. The choice is yours."

4. What about making music as meditation?

Andrew and Sarah were both interested in the answer to this question.

Using music practice as the focus of meditation is nothing new. I have been doing it myself for many years. Any musician, regardless of his or her ability or experience, can use music practice as meditation. What is more, musicians can use meditation as a way to accelerating their progress. The secret is to remain focused during music practice. Practising music as mediation can help a musician play better or sing better. In addition, practising mindfully can also help a musician create a peaceful inner sanctuary. This can be very useful during a demanding performance. Learning how to practice mindfully, with non-judgemental awareness, takes time. We are easily distracted by our own thoughts and emotions. We may think that we will never be able to master a certain technique. We may become irritable about our perceived failure. Mindfully meditating while practising music means that we notice these thoughts but we do not engage emotionally with them. Our ability to concentrate with full awareness while singing or playing improves with practice and over time.

"For me, the practice of meditation – in its more secular usage, the cultivation of mindfulness – has brought an enormous amount to my life and music-making. A sense of clarity and control, less neurosis about ambitions and career, greater efficiency, awareness and body sense as a pianist. As a composer, I'm more in touch with the sources of my own creativity." - Rolf Hind

In the next chapter, we'll discuss breathing meditation, the one meditation method that suits all VAK learners and interpreters. You will also meet Jenny, whose boss Suzie Stressjunkie, is driving Jenny nuts.

Chapter 8

Breathing Meditation

Jenny's phone call

Jenny rang me a week ago. She desperately needs to get away for a few days, preferably for a week or two. Her boss is driving her nuts. Due to the ever-increasing pressure at work and the constant threat of redundancy, the stress is becoming unbearable. She can't remember when she last had time to eat a healthy, nourishing meal. She never has time to do any exercise. Her annual gym membership expires in 2 months and she has only been to the gym once this year. In a moment of weakness, at the end of a particularly hectic and demanding day, she has started smoking again. She knows she is drinking far too much.

To escape the stress at work, Jenny explains that she dreams of sitting quietly next to a placid lake, contently thinking of absolutely nothing. She wants to be far away from never-ending demands and impossible-to-keep dead-lines. She can just about feel the life-giving warmth of the late afternoon sun on her face. She can hear the gentle cooing of a couple of courting doves in an ancient oak tree. She can smell the heady perfume of roses, sweet peas and lilies drifting over the lake towards her. As the late afternoon fades into early evening, she imagines hundreds of candles floating on the lake. She sees the flickering light of the candles gradually eclipse the breathtakingly beautiful sunset colours reflected on the surface of the lake: soft pink, deep ruby and dark reds.

Jenny insists that she needs to get away as soon as possible from the pollution, the heavy traffic on the streets, the mind-numbing commute, the depressing evening news, the frustration at work, the difficult relationships at home. She wants to go somewhere where she can recharge her batteries. She wants to eat healthily, drink pure water, get some exercise and breathe fresh air. She wishes she can find time to work out who she is. She needs to decide what it is she really wants, at this point in her life. She wants to figure out how to get what she wants. She wants to heal from the disappointments life seems to throw at her with unrelenting regularity.

Jenny says that her boss, Suzie Stressjunkie, has just been on a short break in the south of France. Suzie attended an equine-guided experiential learning and meditation workshop. One of our workshops. Jenny says that Suzie talked about our equine-guided personal development holiday incessantly for three weeks. Jenny admitted that she was eventually thoroughly sick of hearing about this miraculous place. Admittedly, Suzie did come back looking fabulous: relaxed, healthy, sun-tanned and happy. According to Suzie, who has been on loads of retreats (lucky Suzie), this one was one of the best she has ever attended. It was quite different from the rest.

What made it so special? Apparently, this was a question that Suzie was eager to answer, at length and in detail whenever asked. Suzie says the setting was "exquisite and exceptional." She stayed in a 200-year-old half-timbered French farmhouse, ancient and authentic. The farmhouse stands on 22 of its own acres in the midst of fertile vineyards, mysterious woods and rolling meadows. It is surrounded by quaint little villages dating from the 12th century, majestic chateaux and stately cathedral towns. It was "incredibly easy" to get there. Suzie managed to get a "ridiculously cheap" ticket from one of the budget airlines that flies to an airport close by. Bordeaux, or Toulouse. There is also a huge lake, as well as 6 natural springs that supply mountain-fresh drinking water... Here Suzie usually interrupts herself to ask if she has mentioned the impressive, snow-capped Pyrenées mountains range, visible from each hilltop?

Jenny says that Suzie still talks a lot about our horses. Jenny feels that she should mention to me that she does not trust horses. Way too big. Way too unpredictable. Way too intimidating. Jenny agreed that they are beautiful creatures, but she prefers to admire them from afar. Very far.

Apart from lazing around on a sunbed, or in a hammock in the shade of an old oak tree or on a bench in the fruit and vegetable garden, Suzie spent a fair amount of time with our Friesian horses. She meditated while watching the horses graze peacefully in a fragrant meadow. She participated in simple exercises with the horses aimed to help participants build self-confidence. The exercises improved their communication skills and helped them to resolve conflict faster. The exercises also helped participants develop more satisfying relationships. They learnt how to handle stress better. Jenny is not altogether sure about this. She is very relieved to hear that even though it is an equine-guided workshop, no riding is required. In fact, no knowledge of horses is required at all. According to Suzie, the retreat leader said that people who are afraid or even scared witless of horses benefit most from the horse exercises. It offers them the opportunity to learn how to challenge their fears, in a safe environment. That does sound like something I might have said.

It is quite clear to Jenny that something has happened to Suzie. Something that has definitely made Jenny's life easier. Suzie is more attentive and easier to talk to. She now actually listens to what people are saying to her. Jenny has been thinking about this ancient French farmhouse...our ancient farmhouse. She wondered if I thought that she might benefit from also attending a workshop here?

Assessing Jenny's problem

I replied to Jenny that if she needs to get away from the endless hustle-and-bustle and ever-more-challenging demands that she faces every day, even if only for a few days, attending a personal empowerment workshop in the sun-blessed south of France might not be such a bad idea. It definitely sounded as if she needed a break and if she could, at the same time as she recharged her batteries, pick up some useful stress management skills, so much the better.

A few good reasons why Jenny might benefit from coming here came to mind:

- It would allow Jenny to experience the slower pace of life in the French countryside. People here know how to appreciate the simple pleasures of life: good food, good wine, good company. Our farm is located deep in the heart of rural France, in a region as yet unspoilt by international tourism. Here the age-old laid-back French way of life is the only way of being. As Suzie so eloquently wrote in her testimonial: "The pace of life slows down dramatically from the moment you arrive at this ancient homestead. The peace won by cultivating and lovingly caring for this patch of land for centuries invades your soul as soon as you step out of the car." Jenny said she finds the fact that the farm has been a place of healing for hundreds (maybe thousands) of years most intriguing. Suzie told her that "the simple beauty of the farmhouse contrasts with the dramatic beauty of the setting and compliments the profound feeling of peace that is at the same time humbling and inspiring." A walking and talking travel brochure, thank you, Suzie!

- Jenny would also enjoy exploring the surrounding area. Situated in its own valley, secluded but not isolated, our farm is nevertheless within easy reach of several spiritual sanctuaries. The most famous one of these is no doubt, Lourdes. Jenny has heard about Lourdes and its miracles. Although she is sceptical, she wouldn't mind checking out the place out for herself. Nor would she mind spending a day luxuriating in one of the spas nearby (Cazaubon, Bagnère-de-Bigorre or Pau.) She thought she might add an extra bed-and-breakfast day to the beginning or to the end of the workshop. To visit Lourdes. Maybe one of the spas as well.

- Coming here from the UK will enable Jenny to avoid getting even more stressed and exhausted by long-distance international travel. According to Suzie, travelling here is easy and inexpensive. Jenny said that she is a bit reluctant to book an exotic holiday to a faraway paradise at the moment. Nearly every day brings news of a new airline disaster or terrorist attack. She would prefer to travel to and in Europe. She has to watch her pennies (don't we all), so she was relieved to hear that both EasyJet and Ryanair fly to airports close by: Toulouse, Bordeaux, Pau, Lourdes and Biarritz. These days even British Airways and Air France offer affordable flights. Another option would be to take the TGV (train). Jenny LOVES train-travel. On the super-fast TGV, train travel is sooooooo affordable and comfortable. The train goes all the way from London or Paris to Mont de Marsan and Auch, from where guests are collected and transferred here.

- Jenny will be able to find out for herself if horses can really be personal development guides. Jenny feels intimidated and curious at the same time. She thinks she could manage the equine-guided meditation sessions led by the herd. She is not so sure about the equine-assisted personal development sessions. She does find it intriguing, though, that some of the workshop hosts are horses! She is interested in the possible improvements (miracles would be needed, really) it may work in her life.

- A few days here would not only help Jenny to rejuvenate mind, body and soul. She would also, just as importantly, learn how to sustain this state of mind once she gets back to her everyday life. Guests can recharge their batteries here, the whole day long if they prefer. They can also learn how to keep their batteries fully charged once they are back home. This has always been Jenny's problem. She said that it usually takes her a couple of days to unwind when she gets to her long-dreamed-about holiday destination. Just when she is fully relaxed and restored, she has to go back. Stepping straight back into the rat-race, within days of her arrival, she is as stressed as she was before she left. Jenny was fascinated to hear that Suzie discovered a way to keep her peace of mind once she returned home. Something to do with "becoming part of the magic of an ancient site of healing, probably dating back to pre-historic times, that now provides shelter and sustenance to modern man" and "you won't believe what I learnt from those horses!"

I did explain to Jenny that our farm is a working farm, in the heart of a farming community. It is not an isolated monastery on a mountaintop. We are within walking distance of three well-known and well-respected wine cellars. In the grape-picking season, one can hear the pickers singing in the vineyards from early in the morning. If it is total silence that she is looking for, then this is not the place to come to. The people of Gascony, as described in Alexander Dumas' book The Three Musketeers, are friendly and hospitable. They love nothing more than stopping for a chat. If you are going for a walk or a bicycle ride, chances are great that you will be hailed by a farmer's wife while digging over her vegetable patch. Or you may have to stop for a chat with a farmer bringing in his cattle. Or you may be greeted by the laughing and joking workers in the vineyards. During this workshop, our guests can interact with people who have mastered the art of living with abundant "joie de vivre," resulting in lasting happiness, better health and exceptional longevity.

So, there are clearly several good reasons why Jenny would benefit from coming to a workshop here, apart from finding out how to handle stress more effectively. If you suffer from stress, attending a retreat could benefit you greatly, here or elsewhere. If you cannot make it here, I would encourage you to look for a retreat closer to home.

During our workshops, one of the meditation methods we introduce participants to is breathing meditation with the horses. Breathing meditation is a very effective stress management strategy and a highly effective stress management strategy is exactly what Jenny needs.

Jenny's Meditation Method: Breathing Meditation

Jenny was still not convinced. She wanted to know:
1. How can breathing meditation reduce stress?
2. What is breathing meditation?
3. How does breathing meditation work?
4. **How can breathing meditation reduce stress?**

Before you can benefit from breathing meditation as a stress management strategy, you must first become aware of your own breathing - an automatic process most of us pay very little attention to on a day-to-day basis. Take a minute or two now and observe how quickly or slowly you are breathing. Is your breathing low (you are breathing from your belly), or high (you are breathing from your chest)? Is there a pause between your in-breath and your out-breath? Do you breathe through your mouth or through your nose? It will be easier to determine your breathing speed and pattern if you put one hand on your chest and the other hand under your bellybutton. This way you can feel which part of your body mostly moves up and down every time you inhale and exhale. Become aware of your breathing in a non-judgemental way – there is no right or wrong way to do this exercise, it is merely about observing what is happening naturally.

This is probably one of the best mindfulness exercises I know, while doing it you are 100% present in the current moment.

This is how our workshop participants start each mindfully breathing exercise with our horses. I first ask them to become aware of their own breathing, without trying to regulate it in any way. They may be breathing slightly faster than normal – if they have never been in the presence of a herd, it is perfectly normal to feel somewhat anxious.

When we are anxious, we change the way we breathe, without realising. Both our breathing rate and pattern change. Instead of taking deep breaths, into our lower lungs, we start to breathe superficially. We take quick, shallow breaths, into our upper lungs only. It feels as if we cannot breathe and we say that we cannot "catch our breath." This expression is not entirely accurate, because we manage perfectly well to breathe in, even if only in short, sharp breaths. The problem is that we do not breathe out properly, we also breathe out in short gasps. This can lead to a condition called hyperventilation.

When you breathe, you breathe in oxygen and breathe out carbon dioxide. Fast, shallow breathing can cause the carbon dioxide levels in your bloodstream to drop too low. This, in turn, can cause quite a few uncomfortable and alarming symptoms. You may

- Have palpitations – your heart feels as if it is racing – and tightness in your chest or chest pain. This is why panic attacks are often confused with heart attacks.
- Feel lightheaded, weak, faint, dizzy and unable to think straight
- Have tingling or numbness in your fingertips or around your mouth
- Experience a sense of terror, or impending doom or death
- Have a dry mouth and feel sweaty, hot and bothered or you may have chills
- Feel nauseous and have abdominal pain or bloating
- Feel as if you are losing control

If this should happen, you can avoid a full-blown panic attack by mindfully doing the breathing exercises described further below.

Once our workshop participants are fully conscious of their own breathing rhythm and depth, I ask them to pay attention to the horses' breathing speeds and patterns. This accomplished, I encourage them again to notice their own breathing, to find out if there has been a change. They often report that their own breathing slows and becomes deeper as they concentrate on the horses' breathing. They also say that they gradually start to feel more and more relaxed. Many report a profound feeling of connection, with the horses and with each other.

In many ways, Jenny reminds me of myself. I also used to have a stressful job and a hectic lifestyle. I was interested in mindfulness meditation, but never quite found the time to learn more about it. I even used to spell mindfulness wrong. When I finally got around to researching meditation and mindfulness, I made a lot of notes, as you do. I found myself, again and again, writing "mindfullness" instead of mindfulness. I had to keep on correcting myself, despite making a concentrated effort to get it right. As I learnt more about mindfulness, I realised that there might be more to this problem than just an irritating and repetitive misspelling: MIND-FULL-NESS.

Like Jenny's, my mind was indeed full. It was full of hundreds of thoughts all vying for supremacy, at the same time. Little wonder I was getting nowhere fast with my mindfulness studies. I suspected that my mind was objecting to being filled with new ideas and new information, without taking time to reflect on any of it. Without first getting rid of limiting habits that no longer served a purpose. I realised that my subconscious mind was trying to get through to me by means of a frustrating spelling mistake.

I stopped and took stock. I made time to reflect and to start a fledgeling meditation practice. In those early days, I knew next to nothing about the practice of meditation, even though I had read a lot about it. More by luck than by wisdom, I chose breathing meditation as a good place to start. I only found out later what an excellent meditation method it is for beginners.

I chose breathing meditation for a very specific reason. At the time, the work I was doing with my horses was all about breathing. I was learning how one can influence the mental state of a horse, positively or negatively, by breathing. If I breathed fast and agitatedly, the horse reflects my distress in his actions. The opposite is also true, an agitated horse can become more settled if its rider purposefully slows and deepens her breathing. My thoughts often behaved like runaway horses, rushing through my mind at neck-breaking speed, completely out of my control. I thought breathing meditation may be a useful meditation method to try.

Breathing meditation sounded like something I could do and could keep on doing.

2. What is breathing meditation?

I did some research online and found out that breathing meditation is a simple technique. All you have to do is to sit somewhere quiet where you will be undisturbed. You start by concentrating on your breathing. I am not very good at sitting still, so I started doing this while walking slowly in a circle. You start by paying attention to your breathing. You can experiment with different breathing rhythms. If long, slow breaths feel comfortable, take steady and deep breaths. If it doesn't, you can use a different rhythm. The idea is to notice your thoughts while you are concentrating on your breathing, without engaging with these thoughts. You bring your awareness back to your breathing every time a thought distracts you. If you notice that your attention has drifted off, don't worry about. It happens to everyone. Just bring your attention back to your breathing, every time it happens.

This sounds very easy, but it is not. Especially in the beginning.

Once you have found a comfortable breathing rhythm, you pay attention to how the breathing feels in other parts of your body. You can begin by focusing on the area just below your navel. You breathe in and out, and you notice how that area moves and feels. If you don't feel any motion there, just be aware that there is no motion. If you do feel motion, notice if there's any tension or tightness. If there's tension, relax and let the tension go. Tell yourself, I breathe calmness in and I breathe stress out, with each breath. If your breathing feels uneven, concentrate on making it smoother. You then move your attention a bit higher up to a spot just below your rib cage. This is sometimes called the solar plexus. Repeat the same process with different parts of your body until you have scanned and removed stress from your whole body. Finally, let your awareness fill your entire body, from the top of your head down to the tips of your toes. Keep your awareness expanded like this for as long as you can. This is difficult, one's awareness tends to shrink to a single spot whenever it can. Think of breathing in and out with your whole body. Let your awareness linger there for a while and then become aware of your surroundings again.

Equine-facilitated Mindfulness Meditation

I started by setting ten minutes out of every day apart to do mindful breathing. As there are few days in my life as the owner of 5 horses that I have ten minutes to spare, I often did it while I was with one or more of our horses. I walked in a circle in the barn, with the horses munching away at their hay nearby. I did my mindful breathing right there. I started by concentrating on my breathing. Breathing in and out. My thoughts initially continued to rush around in my head. Time and again I had to remind myself to concentrate on my breathing. This did get easier as time went by. In the first few weeks, the horses paid me no attention whatsoever. This is perfectly normal. When our horses are eating, they pay little attention to anything else.

The strange thing is, after a few weeks, at the end of the ten minutes, I would open my eyes and find a horse standing nearby. He or she would stand there, dozing contentedly, head down and eyes closed. It was not always the same horse. Sometimes it was a mare, sometimes a gelding, even on occasion the stallion. More and more often I would open my eyes and find a horse, closer and closer. One morning, I felt a gentle breath on my cheek. When I opened my eyes, Belle was standing right in front of me, with her head nearly in my lap. Her daughter Aurore was napping (or meditating?) next to her.

These days, at the end of each meditation, when I open my eyes and I see our gorgeous, contented and totally relaxed horses before me, I feel intensely grateful. I think bringing gratitude to the practice of meditation makes it extra valuable. I always spend a couple of moments thanking God for all the blessings in my life.

I never had any problems with the spelling of mindfulness again.

As with every new skill one wants to master, you have to meditate regularly. You have to keep going to get the full benefit. That is why I chose ten minutes of breathing meditation a day for Jenny. It would only take ten minutes, although it might initially feel much longer! She could do it anytime she had a few moments free. She wouldn't need any special equipment like candles, mats or bells. She could do it anywhere she could find a quiet spot where she wouldn't be disturbed. Of course, it is essential that she remembers to mute her phone! I suspect that breathing meditation is the meditation method that she is most likely to keep up in the long run. She agreed that she could probably manage to do ten minutes of this every day for the rest of her life. Maybe breathing meditation could also suit you?

3. How does Breathing Meditation work?

There are various ways you can practise breathing meditation. One of the most popular methods is alternate nostril breathing. This is how you do it:

Exercise 1

Bring your right hand (if you are right-handed) towards your forehead. Rest your index finger and your middle finger between your eyebrows. The fingers you use alternatively to block one of your nostrils are your thumb and your ring finger.

Start by taking a deep breath in and out through both your nostrils.

Close your right nostril with your right thumb. Inhale slowly through the left nostril.

Close the left nostril with your ring finger so both nostrils are closed. Hold your breath for a few seconds.

Release your right nostril and breathe out slowly through your right nostril. Pause for a few seconds.

Inhale slowly through the right nostril.

Hold both nostrils closed (with ring finger and thumb), then release and exhale slowly through the left nostril.

Repeat the cycle ten times.

Exercise 2

Another breathing method I find very useful during meditation, but also in stressful situations, is square breathing. This method is even simpler than alternate nostril breathing. It can be combined with alternate nostril breathing. All you do is:

Breathe in while counting to four.

Hold your breath while counting to four.

Breathe out while counting to four.

Hold while counting to four.

If your attention drifts off, try focusing on a different colour during each of the four stages. Blue when you breathe in, white when you hold, green when you breathe out and yellow when you hold. There is a large variety of breathing patterns that can be used during breathing meditation. I include these two here because I find them the most useful. Breathing meditation can be a meditation method on its own, or it can be a preliminary exercise before moving on to another meditation method.

Exercise 3

Sit or lie down in a comfortable position. Imagine your lungs are divided into three parts. Breathe in gently through your nose. First, imagine the lowest part of your lungs filling with air. Next, imagine the middle part of your lungs filling with air and then your lungs filling with air right to the top. Relax your shoulders. Gently and slowly exhale fully and completely. Repeat the exercise three or four times.

Exercise 4

Resting the tip of your tongue against the roof of your mouth, right behind your top front teeth. Keep your tongue in place throughout the practice. Start by exhaling completely through your mouth. Next, close your mouth, inhaling silently through your nose as you count to four in your head. Then, for seven seconds, hold your breath. Exhale from your mouth for eight seconds. This is called 4-7-8 breathing. Repeat at least 4 times. The held breath (for seven seconds) is the most critical part of this practice.

In the beginning, you may prefer to listen to a guided breathing meditation. Beginners often feel that they relax more easily when they listen to a guided meditation on YouTube. They only have to concentrate on what the voice is telling them to do. I use guided meditations too.

Sometimes I feel less motivated to meditate than other times. At times like these, a guided meditation comes in very useful. I play it on my laptop if I am inside, on my phone if I am outside.

Breathing meditation works for all VAK preferences. You can download a variety of excellent breathing meditation scripts to help you master the basic method.

"Breath is the bridge which connects life to consciousness, which unites your body to your thoughts." Thích Nhat Hanh

Chapter 9

Contemplative Meditation

Nix's letter

"Hi Margaretha,

Nicola here, or Nix, for short. I am a travel blogger. I saw recently that a lot of travel bloggers follow you. I saw that you follow a fair amount of travel bloggers on Twitter. I also saw that you often re-tweet other travel bloggers' tweets. I thought I would follow you too. That is how I found out about your workshops.

I am now heading for your part of the world. I wondered if I could come and do a working holiday at your place. I am crazy about horses as well as about France, so I really cannot imagine a better place to spend a week or two.

On your website, you ask people who want to come and do a working holiday with you to tell you a bit more about themselves. You also ask that applicants should tell you why they are interested in working meditation.

Well, I used to be a very good girl. Not so much anymore. I lived up to my parents' expectations. After school, I got myself a decent degree. I started working in an office and I got my big toe onto the corporate ladder. I didn't get any further in the next two years. In January 2012, I had had enough. I resigned from my job and I started travelling. My money soon ran out so I had to find a way to earn a living. I started my travel blog in February 2012 and today I make enough money from it to fund my travels. Most of my earnings come from advertisements on my blog itself. I also earn a bit from social media consulting and managing, from sponsored social media campaigns and from sponsored blog posts. I get the occasional paid press trip.

When I first had a look at your website, I decided that I absolutely wanted to come and do a workshop with you. I have a problem, though. Even though my income has substantially increased since I started specialising in solo female travel, with a dog, I still do not earn enough to be able to afford to a mindfulness meditation workshop. I subscribed to your blog. I drooled over each new post about the horses. I loved finding out more about the part of France you live in. I am very glad I did! Subscribe to your blog, I mean. Otherwise, I would never have known about the working holidays that you mentioned in last September's email.

You working holidays would be absolutely perfect for me for two reasons. Firstly, because it only calls for minimal financial investment. Secondly, because meditation is something I am getting more and more interested in, the longer and the further I travel. I have travelled through several Eastern countries. That was where I first picked up the habit. I have been practising meditation now for nearly three years. It has helped me cope with the unexpected challenges of travelling. It has helped me deal with the financial uncertainty my lifestyle generates. I would say I am pretty good at it.

Assessing Nix's Problem

The last year or so, I have started to ask myself a lot of questions. I have discovered that nearly all religions use some or other form of meditation. I had a Christian upbringing. I wanted to learn more about Christian meditation, so I stayed for two weeks at a monastery. That is how I discovered contemplative meditation. I want to learn more about it. If you know something about contemplative meditation that you can share with me while I do my working holiday at your place, I would be seriously grateful.

I started travelling when I was twenty-five, I am now twenty-nine. In a couple of months, I will be thirty years old. Time to take stock, I think. Time to make decisions about the future. Where better to do this than in the south of France while learning more about a subject as important to me as mindfulness meditation? Surrounded by Friesian horses, without doubt, the most beautiful breed of horses currently known to man!

I am fit as a fiddle. I run whenever I can. I saw that you are a runner too! I do yoga daily. Working in exchange for my board, lodging and instruction will be no problem. I do travel with my dog, Tara, but she is very well behaved. She will be perfectly content to sleep in a barn. She gets on well with other dogs and cats... and horses!

Please say that you have an opening for us. I promise you will not regret it.

Hopefully, à très bientot,
  Nix."

"Dear Nix,

Indeed, I remember connecting with you on Twitter a good nine months ago. I also follow your blog. I enjoy seeing the places you have visited through your eyes. I must congratulate you on the quality of your posts and the professional approach you take to blogging. Little wonder you have more than fifty thousand followers!

Of course you are welcome to come here for a working holiday. Tara is welcome too. I suspect she will get on famously with our own dog, a Belgian Sheppard–New Foundland cross called Melchi'or. The cats too, they may be small, but they are ferocious. They do not take any nonsense from dogs, other cats...or horses!

We receive quite a few applications every year from working holiday hopefuls. We rarely take more than one or two candidates per year. We select these very carefully. As we already know each other, I have no reservations about accepting you. On the contrary, I think it will be tremendous fun to have you here.

Nix's Meditation Choice: Contemplative Christian Meditation

About contemplative meditation: Yes, I know a fair amount about it, and I am willing to share my knowledge with you. There is one thing I need to mention. As I am a Christian, my knowledge about contemplative meditation is intertwined with my religious beliefs. Our workshops, though, are non-denominational. People from all, any and no religious convictions come here to attend workshops. As our workshops are not associated with any specific religion, I do not teach contemplative meditation during our workshops. Mostly because I do not think I can separate contemplative meditation from my Christian beliefs. For me, contemplative meditation is Christian meditation. As long as you are okay with that, I am happy to share with you what I know. We can investigate further by answering the following questions:

1. What is Contemplative Christian Meditation?
2. How does one meditate contemplatively?

You have probably already had a look at the definition of Christian contemplative meditation on Wikipedia: "Christian meditation is a form of prayer in which a structured attempt is made to become aware of and reflect upon the revelations of God. Christian meditation is the process of deliberately focusing on specific phrases (such as a bible passage) and reflecting on their meaning in the context of the love of God. Both the Eastern and Western Christian churches have emphasised the use of Christian meditation as an element in increasing one's knowledge of Christ." Christians receive clear instructions about meditation:

"Whatever is true, whatever is honourable, whatever is right, whatever is pure, whatever is lovely, whatever is of good repute, if there is any excellence and if anything worthy of praise, dwell on these things" Philippians 4:8

1. What is Contemplative Christian Meditation?

Christian contemplative meditation is about pondering God's revealed truths and reflecting on how they apply to us. Even in the Old Testament, David encourages his readers to meditate, "I meditate on your precepts and consider your ways. I delight in your decrees; I will not neglect your word." (Ps. 119:15-16) In his book, "Satisfy Your Soul," Dr Bruce Demarest writes, "A quieted heart is our best preparation for all this work of God...Meditation refocuses us from ourselves and from the world so that we reflect on God's Word, His nature, His abilities, and His works...So we prayerfully ponder, muse, and 'chew' the words of Scripture....The goal is simply to permit the Holy Spirit to activate the life-giving Word of God."

Christians have been meditating for nearly two thousand years. The way contemplative Christian meditation is practised changed a lot over the years. In the fourth century AD, Christian meditation was based on the "lectiodivina." Lectio divina means "sacred reading." It consists of four stages: "lectio" (reading), "meditatio" (meditation), "oratio" (prayer) and "contemplatio" (contemplation). In the lectio (reading) stage, you choose a passage from the Bible. You read it slowly and deliberately. During the next stage, meditatio (meditation), you ponder the text. In the oratio (prayer) stage, you talk to God about what you have read, asking Him to reveal the truth contained in the specific passage you read. During the final stage, contemplatio (contemplation) stage, you simply rest in the Lord's presence.

According to Saint Padre Pio (1887–1968), "the person who meditates and turns his mind to God, who is the mirror of his soul, seeks to know his faults, tries to correct them, moderates his impulses, and puts his conscience in order." He adds, "Through the study of books one seeks God; by meditation one finds him."

Saint Teresa of Avila says about Christian meditation, "We begin by thinking of the favour which God bestowed upon us by giving us His only Son and we do not stop there but proceed to consider the mysteries of His whole glorious life. Christian meditation involves looking back on Jesus' life. It involves thanksgiving and it involves adoration of God for his action in sending Jesus for human salvation."

Today, the Catholic Church defines meditation as a form of prayer: "Meditation is above all a quest. The mind seeks to understand the why and how of the Christian life, in order to adhere and respond to what the Lord is asking" (Catechism section # 2705).

Christian meditation differs essentially from Eastern meditation (Hinduism, Buddhism, Jainism, Daoism) in that eastern meditation is practised with the purpose of transcending the mind and attaining enlightenment. Christian meditation aims for a deeper understanding of the Bible and a closer intimacy with God.

2. How does one meditate contemplatively?

There are various options.

Christians believe that contemplative meditation should be an active thought process whereby Christians study verses or passages in the Bible, pray about these verses and ask God to give them understanding through the Holy Spirit. They then put what they have learnt into practice as they go about their daily activities. Christians believe that one should not "just listen to God's word. You must do what it says. Otherwise, you are only fooling yourselves. For if you listen to the word and don't obey, it is like glancing at your face in a mirror. You see yourself, walk away, and forget what you look like. But if you look carefully into the perfect law that sets you free, and if you do what it says and don't forget what you heard, then God will bless you for doing it." NLT James 1:22

Rick Warren, in "The Purpose Driven Life," an excellent book that I highly recommend, describes meditation as "focused thinking. It takes serious effort. You select a verse and reflect on it over and over in your mind...If you know how to worry, you already know how to meditate." Warren says, "No other habit can do more to transform your life and make you more like Jesus than daily reflection on Scripture...If you look up all the times God speaks about meditation in the Bible, you will be amazed at the benefits He has promised to those who take the time to reflect on His Word throughout the day."

I shortly discuss four options below:
- Christian Loving Kindness Meditation
- Centering Prayer
- Mantra Meditation
- Gratitude Meditation

Christian Loving Kindness Meditation

As Christians, we have been taught to love others as ourselves - "A new commandment I give to you, that you love one another: just as I have loved you, you also are to love one another." (John 13:34) But how do we put this into practice, especially if we don't particularly like, never mind love, ourselves? The loving kindness meditation can help us learn how to love ourselves as well as others.

As you know by now, during a loving-kindness practice, the practitioner extends good wishes to various people including and starting with him/herself: "May I be safe. May I be happy. May I be healthy. May I be free from suffering." The Christian take on this may be "May I know God's love. May I know God's rest. May I know God's peace." The practice of loving-kindness consists of sending love, compassion, peace and joy to ourselves, to those we love, to those toward whom we are indifferent, to those with whom we have difficulties or who are our enemies, and finally to all people and beings everywhere: "May you know God's love. May you know God's rest. May you know God's peace."

Let's start with ourselves. Create an image of yourself in your mind, visualise yourself (more about this in the chapter about visualisation) – as you would like to be: happy, healthy and blessed. Imagine yourself safe in God's loving arms.

May I experience God's love.
May I experience God's rest.
May I experience God's peace.

You can add whatever currently troubles you: "May I be able to cope with this difficult situation. May I be filled with loving kindness towards myself. May I be able to face this illness with courage and patience."

Now extend this blessing to someone you love: your partner, your best friend, a family member, someone who fills you with feelings of love, tenderness and happiness. Visualise this person in your mind's eye. Imagine this person happy, prosperous and healthy. Remember happy times together. You might want to help with something specific in your friend's life. Perhaps they're having money worries or problems with a partner. You can add these things to our phrases: "May you be free from debt. May you and your partner be happy together. May you have the strength and courage to cope with this illness."

May this person experience God's love.

May this person experience God's rest.

May this person experience God's peace.

Next, you do exactly the same with someone you feel indifferent about: an acquaintance or even a stranger.

Now comes the hard part! Let us now extend this blessing to someone whom you just don't get on with. Practising loving-kindness towards difficult people or enemies enables you, when someone acts in a hurtful or disrespectful way toward you, to send him a blessing instead of a curse. For instance, if someone cuts in front of you in heavy traffic, you do not swear at him. Instead, you pray that he arrives safely and does not harm anyone. Imagine a person that you do not get on with, or who has treated you unfairly, and try to extend feelings of kindness and compassion towards this person. If feelings of anger arise, release these feelings to God, by just letting go.

May they experience God's love.

May they experience God's rest.

May they experience God's peace.

Finally, you extend God's blessing to all beings, everywhere. As a horsewoman, I always include my own horses, as well as all other horses, in this blessing. My cats too - in fact, all animals, all plants, the whole earth and all its inhabitants can be included in this blessing. All that is, all that has ever been made, all that is and was and is to come: all held by God, sustained by God's love and blessed by God.

   May all beings everywhere experience God's love.

   May all beings everywhere experience God's rest.

   May all beings everywhere experience God's peace.

Centering Prayer

In 1974, Father William Meninger dusted off an old book in the monastery library at St. Joseph Abbey in Spencer, Massachusetts. He read it. The book was called "The Cloud of Unknowing." It was an anonymous 14th-century manual on contemplative meditation. It was written in Middle English, the language of Chaucer. In the book, an older monk is writing to a novice, instructing him in contemplative meditation: "This is what you are to do. Lift your heart up to the Lord with a gentle stirring of love, desiring him for his own sake and not for his gifts."

Father Meninger began teaching this method to priests who came on retreat at the abbey. "I have to confess," Meninger says, "that when I first started teaching it, I did not think it could be taught to laypeople, but didn't take long before I began to realise that this was not just for monks and priests, but for everybody." Father William's abbot, Father Thomas Keating, has spread the method widely. It is now known as "centering prayer."

Centering Prayer is practised as follows:

   Sit comfortably with your eyes closed, relax your body and quiet your mind.

   Choose a sacred word that best supports your sincere intention to be in God's presence and open yourself to His divine action within you. The idea is to contemplate God's presence.

   Let that word be the symbol of your sincere intention to be in God's presence.

Whenever you become aware of anything (thoughts, feelings, perceptions, images, associations, etc.), simply return to your sacred word. Father Meninger calls it a "prayer word." He says, "This is your defence against abstract thoughts, your defence against distraction."

Father Thomas Keating writes, "The method consists in letting go of every kind of thought during prayer, even the most devout thoughts." Although the practice makes use of a "sacred word," Fr. Keating emphasises that Centering Prayer is not an exercise in concentrating, or focusing one's attention on something (such as a mantra - see below), but rather is concerned with intention.

Mantra Meditation

There is another form of meditation that Christians practice, closely related to the modern Western idea of meditation. It is a form of focused meditation, involving repeating a single word over and over. A word like "Maranatha" for example. Maranatha means "Come, Lord" in Aramaic. It can be found in the New Testament. Another option is to repeat the Jesus Prayer "Lord Jesus Christ, Son of God, have mercy on me, a sinner," while meditating. The idea is not to repeat the phrase mindlessly but to use it as a focal point to keep one's mind from wandering aimlessly.

Gratitude Meditation

Contemplating everything that you have to be grateful for, thanking God and praising Him for his generosity is a meditation that very effectively helps me to cope with my own personal challenges. I think that expressing gratitude is the most effective way to invite God to work miracles in your life. I did so in a blog post called "Gratitude Prayer" in the not too distant past. I am not the only one who is convinced of this simple truth:

"A thankful heart is one of the primary identifying characteristics of a believer. It stands in stark contrast to pride, selfishness and worry. And it helps fortify the believer's trust in the Lord and reliance of His provision, even in the toughest times. No matter how choppy the seas become, a believer's heart is buoyed by constant praise and gratefulness to the Lord." –John MacArthur

The problem is, in difficult situations, it is not always easy to give thanks. I find Tony Evans's approach helpful, "God says to give thanks IN everything. That doesn't mean you need to give thanks FOR everything. You don't need to give thanks for that bad day. Or for that bad relationship. Or being passed over at work. Financial hardship. Whatever it is – you are not to give thanks FOR the difficulties, but rather IN the difficulties. That is a very important distinction, and one I think we often miss. Giving thanks IN everything shows a heart of faith that God is bigger than the difficulties and that He can use them, if you approach Him with the right heart and spirit, for your good and His glory."

Matthew Henry gives us an example, "I thank Thee first because I was never robbed before; second, because although they took my purse, they did not take my life; third, although they took my all, it was not much; and fourth, because it was I who was robbed and not I who robbed."

So, "Do not be anxious about anything, but in everything by prayer and supplication with thanksgiving let your requests be made known to God." Phil 4:6. Below, an example of a gratitude prayer that you can pray right now: Lord, teach me to offer you a heart of thanksgiving and praise in all my daily experiences of life. Teach me to be joyful always, to pray continually and to give thanks in all my circumstances. I praise You, Lord. Amen.

Gratitude is the foundation of everything I share during our Connect with Horses Personal Empowerment workshops, I devote a whole chapter of this book to it. You can read more about its exceptional benefits in the chapter: Gratitude Meditation.

Combining Contemplative Meditation with Working Meditation

If you come here on a working holiday, Nix, you will have the opportunity to learn more about the meditation methods I cover during the workshops: writing meditation, music meditation, walking meditation, visualisation meditation, working meditation and of course equine-guided meditation. You can also attend some of the mindfulness field trips: the trip to the fresh food market, the wine tasting trip and the Santiago de Compostelle Pilgrim's route walk, as long as you put in the working meditation hours required. We can discuss contemplative meditation together, at the end of the day.

I think our "working meditation holiday" page on the website explains the set-up in great detail. If you have any further questions, just let me know.

Yours,
  Margaretha."

In the next chapter, I discuss a very powerful meditation method: visualisation meditation - used extensively today by athletes, actors, politicians, doctors...in fact, by loads of people daily to enable them to live happier, healthier and more successful lives.

Chapter 10

Visualisation Meditation

Patricia's Letter

"Dear Margaretha,

I have read your book "Self-confidence made Simple - 16 French Women Share their Self-esteem Secrets." I have found that we have a lot of things in common. Like you, I am in my 49th year. I have had a few problems coming to terms with the fact that I am now middle-aged. I have found the links to the various blogs, groups and websites for midlife women in your book of great value. It has proved to me that I am not the only one who feels like this. I have made a few good friends in one of the Facebook groups you mentioned, The Women of Midlife. I have received excellent advice. I found answers to most of my questions about the menopause. Like you, I also have a few problems with my health. Like you, I have arrived at a stage in my life where I am considering radical changes. I saw on your website that you are doing two Radical Midlife Renaissance Retreats this year. I could come to either, but the one in July would suit me best.

I am familiar with classical meditation. I started a sitting meditation practice three years ago when I was diagnosed with breast cancer. It has helped me cope with the challenges the diagnosis presented. It also helped with the treatment that followed. My story is the same as most other women's. I found a small lump. Once I managed to get enough courage together to talk to my doctor about it, she immediately arranged a mammogram. The mammogram revealed a suspicious lump. The biopsy confirmed that it was cancer. I was lucky. The complementary tests showed no evidence that it had spread. I had a mastectomy followed by chemotherapy. I have not had any further problems. Writing it all down like this, just the cold, hard facts, feels strange. It does, however, help me to distance myself from the pain, suffering and insecurity that was part of my life.

I am grateful that I have survived. I am also very proud of the fact. I think that it has made me a better person. It has taught me to value every day that I am alive. It has crystallised an idea that I have been playing with for some time now. I am stuck in a dead-end job, much as you were before you left medicine to retrain in horse psychotherapy. Your description of how you managed to make this enormous change has given me hope that I may be able to do the same. Cancer has taught me that there is no time left to waste doing something that you no longer enjoy. Or get any satisfaction from.

My personal circumstances also changed dramatically. I got divorced. My husband could not (or would not) put up with the strain of all the hospital visits. He could not handle the uncertainty. He could not cope with the side-effects of the treatment... Ironically, I think it was the loss of my hair that was the final death blow to an already faltering marriage. Apparently, not all that many marriages survive breast cancer. I no longer hate him for leaving me when I needed him most. I have moved on. I now want to make the most of the years that I have left.

That is why I am writing to you today.

I have always considered myself a strong woman. I have always been able to set myself goals. I always worked hard until I reached my targets.

I have decided that a change of career is essential to my continued well-being. Until I developed the breast cancer, I was employed by a large accountancy firm in the city. I did a job that paid my share of the bills, fairly generously, but it was not a job I particularly enjoyed. I have been doing the same job, more or less, for many years. There was no further possibility of advancement. I have always had a dream. Please don't laugh, I realise it is pretty far-fetched. I dream of owning a tea shop that also sells books. I imagine that customers will come into my bookshop and look through the books on the shelves. They may pick up a few and then sit down to a cup of tea or coffee, with a piece of home-made cake, while they decide which books they would like to buy. I have always enjoyed baking, although I am not a keen cook. Cakes are different. I love all sorts of cakes. I love decadently delicious chocolate cakes, mouth-watering Black forest cakes drenched in cherry liqueur, French fruit tarts made from the freshest apples, raspberries or apricots and delicately tiered Viennese tortes. I would definitely qualify as yet another crazy cupcake lady. I am thoroughly addicted to decorating cupcakes! I am also a coffee connoisseur and a tea aficionado. I would love to offer a large variety of both at my bookshop. As they say, life is too short to drink bad coffee. Same goes for tea, I think.

I have been a bookworm since I mastered the art of reading. Books have always offered me an escape when life got too demanding. I read everything: crime, mystery, romance, non-fiction, horror and women's fiction. Anything I can lay my hands on. Recently I have also started reading a fair number of e-books. That is how I came across yours. I prefer to hold a real book in my hands, turn the pages and smell the paper. I was relieved to see your book is also available in print. I admit it. I prefer old-fashioned books to e-books. I think there are enough people who feel the same to make my bookshop dream a viable possibility. Of course, I will not object if someone wants to come in and read their e-books on a reading device while having a cup of my irresistible Blue Mountain coffee and a slice of my unforgettable

Death-by-Chocolate cake!

My problem is that I just can't take the plunge. My illness may well have shown me how important it is to make the most of each day, but it has also left me feeling vulnerable. I know I can do this. I have been planning it for years. I have some savings that I could use. I am an experienced accountant. I have helped many people set up and run successful businesses. I just cannot, for the life of me, make myself leave the suffocating security of my current job.

I thought that coming on a midlife renaissance retreat in my all-time favourite country would be helpful. I would like to discuss my problem with you and maybe with some of the other women on the retreat. This might provide me with the confidence and the motivation to set all this in motion. I am quite intrigued by the equine-assisted side of things too. I have read that you and your horses have done some outstanding work in helping women with breast cancer.

Let me know if that sounds workable.

All the best,
   Patricia Woods."

Assessing Patricia's Problem

I thought that Patricia's planned career change sounded feasible. Having gone through the same nerve-racking process, I fully under-stood her reluctance to leave a well-paid job for the insecurity of self-employment. Especially as her plan would involve a substantial financial investment. More and more women make drastic changes during midlife. She was certainly not part of a misguided minority. There is a lot of guidance and support available online from women who have survived the challenges of such changes. With her experience of helping others start and run businesses, Patricia had a very good chance of making a success of it.

But how to help her overcome her natural reluctance to leave her comfort zone? She was already familiar with meditation as a practice, so I decided I might be able to build on this foundation. I invited her to come to the July retreat that year.

I have long been an enthusiastic believer in visualisation. I have used visualisation during meditation to help patients handle stress, cope with pain, lose weight and speed up healing. Patricia could use visualisation meditation to rebuild her self-esteem. She could also use it to mentally rehearse her desired outcome, running her bookshop.

During the retreat, I explained to Patricia that I often use visualisation myself when faced with a challenging situation. I rehearse the ideal outcome in my mind before I start the task. More often than not, this has a positive influence on the result. She was keen to find out more about it. First, she wanted to know:

1. What is Visualisation Meditation? She also wanted to know:
2. How do I practice visualisation meditation?

Patricia's Meditation Method: Visualisation Meditation

1. What is Visualisation Meditation?

It is useful to distinguish between Simple Visualisation and Creative Visualisation during meditation. Simple visualisation involves seeing an image in your mind's eye, for example, a horse grazing peacefully when you want to relax. Creative visualisation has more to do with creating something new. For example, if you want to lose weight, you could visualise a happy, fit and healthy you at your desired weight.

- Simple Visualisation

One of the most popular applications of simple visualisation during meditation is relaxation. I thought this would be particularly helpful to Patricia once she started making changes. I usually recommend that people start by focusing on their breathing, to still their minds. Patricia would already be familiar with this technique. The next step is to picture a peaceful scene, place, colour or image. For example, you can imagine that you are watching a glorious sunset on a deserted beach, or that you are walking through a quiet forest just after the rain or that you are floating on a cloud over a peaceful meadow. If you love books, like Patricia, you may imagine that you are alone in an enormous library. If you love horses as I do, you can simply imagine being in their presence. It works best if you choose your scene, place, colour or picture before you start meditating. Starting a new business is a challenging undertaking. I suggested Patricia adds simple visualisation to her meditative practice. It would empower her to cope with the stress that may come her way, once she starts working on realising her dream.

- Creative visualisation

Creative visualisation is an extremely powerful tool. It can improve your self-image, increase your self-confidence and help you handle difficult and challenging situations. It's a technique used by athletes, writers, psychologists, entrepreneurs and successful people from all walks of life. It has been the subject of self-help books that have sold millions of copies. Napoleon Hill's book, Think and Grow Rich, was probably one of the first. W. Clement Stone said, "Whatever the mind of man can conceive and believe, it can achieve...with a positive mental attitude." I agree with this, basically, but only up to a certain point. The process is somewhat more complicated than just that.

Every day, through the language you use and images you create of yourself in your mind's eye, you develop and adjust your self-image. This influences your interaction with the world around you. It determines your reactions in situations that you find yourself in. You can change the way that you interpret and interact with the world around you. All you need to do is change the way you think about yourself, your strengths, your weaknesses, your opportunities and your limitations.

And you can do it during meditation. During the workshop, Patricia spent most of her time perfecting this meditation method.

2. How do I practice visualisation meditation?

Visualisation is not necessarily meditation. Visualisation can be incorporated into meditation. Patricia already knew that meditation is a state of intense concentration. It focuses the mind by observing without reacting to the endless stream of thoughts that constantly runs through most people's minds. Your focus can be on your breath or on the sensations in your body. Or you can concentrate on repeating a mantra. You also can focus on a specific static or moving object. Patricia preferred to focus on her breathing - the sensation of air entering and leaving her body. She repeated the phrase, "Breathe in healing, breathe out worry" during her illness. I suggested she now change this to, "Breathe in confidence, breathe out stress."

When the focus of your meditation is an image, the meditation can become visualisation. Visualisation is a specific kind of meditation. It is sometimes called mental imagery or mental rehearsal during meditation. It does not have to be a static image, in fact, it rarely is. It usually involves visualising yourself doing something. The idea is to experience the action, the internal and external sensations and the consequences of the action, in great detail, in your mind. From Patricia's e-mail, I already knew that she was good at visualisation.

The paragraph in which she describes her passion for books and baking had my mouth watering. Some people insist that they are no good at visualisation. This is rarely an accurate impression. Most of us are extremely good at visualising impending catastrophes. We usually call it worrying.

Visualisation meditation might start with a mental image of a relaxing place. A place that feels safe and secure. Visualisation for healing might include visualising a healing light bathing the body. Visualisation for athletic peak performance involves seeing and feeling the body perform as perfectly as possible.

Patricia's VARK test showed a strong preference for visual learning with a secondary preference for learning by reading and writing. Visualisation meditation would be perfect for her. I reminded her of Dr Norman Vincent Peale's words, "Formulate and stamp indelibly on your mind a mental picture of yourself as succeeding. Hold this picture tenaciously and never permit it to fade. Your mind will seek to develop this picture!"

- Preparation

To incorporate visualisation into meditation, Patricia needed to do a bit of preparation beforehand. She first and foremost wanted to improve the image of her new self, a cancer survivor at midlife. I usually start by suggesting that guests think about how they are seeing themselves now. I ask them, "Are you convinced that you are a good-for-nothing underachiever that will never amount to anything? Or have you been told so many times that you are incompetent that you are now convinced that you are? Or maybe in the past, you have failed at certain challenges that you have set yourself. Now you firmly believe that you will never succeed in that field. Do you have beliefs that may have served some purpose in the past? These beliefs are no longer useful and are keeping you from making progress. Or have you set yourself certain limitations to protect yourself in the past that are no longer needed?" Most of us do this.

I said to Patricia, "You know, your self-image is directly responsible for your current situation. If you want to improve your current situation, you need to change the way you think about yourself. You need to identify unhelpful beliefs and unrealistic expectations. You need to change the way you talk to yourself. You need to stop saying you cannot take the plunge. Start saying to yourself that you are an intelligent, highly-qualified and experienced survivor. You are able to do this and make a raging success of it.

This is something that you desire to accomplish with all your heart. You believe in this dream. How do you expect to make your dream come true if you keep telling yourself that it is too risky, that you might fail and that you may end up destitute? Tell yourself that whatever comes your way, you are intelligent enough and you have enough resources to handle it."

When you meditate, you may, like Patricia, notice that you sometimes become critical of yourself. Your inner critic might want to convince you that what you have decided to do is too dangerous. The idea is to notice these thoughts, to acknowledge them, but not to react impulsively. You can focus your attention instead on visualising yourself as successful at whatever you have chosen to do. Your inner critic can sabotage your best efforts, that is why I wrote a whole chapter about it in Self-confidence made Simple: 16 French Women Share their Self-esteem Secrets.

- Practice

Once she got the hang of it, there was no stopping Patricia. She visualised her bookshop. She visualised the books on the shelves, even the titles of the books. She visualised the antique tables and chairs, the comfortable armchairs, the wood-burner in the fireplace, the spiral steps up to the second floor and a tiny kitchen with everything to hand. She imagined breathing in the smell of hundreds of old, not-so-old and brand-new books, of freshly-brewed coffee and of beeswax wood polish. She imagined hearing the doorbell tinkle as customers came in. She saw herself settling her customers at a table, taking their order, advising them about the books she thought they would like. She imagined basking in their compliments about her baking, her excellent coffee, her choice of teas, her great idea to open the sort of bookshop they had always been looking for. She imagined doing her books, smiling at the healthy profits her books were showing. She imagined famous authors dropping in for a chat, for a book signing or to pick up a rare book she had managed to find for them. She imagined herself locking up the shop at the end of the day, tired but happy, greeting the neighbouring shopkeepers before she climbed the stairs to her heavenly little flat above the shop. I encouraged her to use all her senses during this exercise, including touch and taste, so she imagined holding some of her most precious books in her hands and tasting of the minute piece of chocolate cake she allowed herself at teatime.

Patricia visualised herself accepting an annual best business woman's award.

It is important to take on board that visualisation, even during meditation, is not enough to create change. Concrete steps need to be taken to realise a desired outcome. If you want to lose weight, as well as visualisation, you will also need to watch your diet and maybe get more exercise.

Visualisation works more effectively when our expectations are realistic. We actually need to believe that we can realise what we are visualising. Sometimes it is better to visualise small achievements one by one on the way to the desired outcome, rather than the end result. Especially if we doubt that we will ever be able to live up to such an enormous challenge.

Visualisation during meditation can function as a way to introduce us to the power of our own minds. It can help you use your mind to its full capacity. Specifically, your right brain. Apparently, our right brain can process 1 billion units of information per second. Our right brain is the creative part of our brain. Visualisation is a creative activity and as such happens in our right brain. What is more, our subconscious mind mainly communicates with us through our right brain. That is why visualisation is an effective way of communicating with our subconscious mind. It is your subconscious mind that is going to help you or hinder you in making your dreams come true.

I have collected a good number of articles about visualisation at Margaretha's Muse on Pinterest. Have a look and let me know what you think about visualisation meditation! on margarethamontagu@gmail.com.

Equine-assisted Personal Development

Patricia also attended a couple of equine-assisted experiential learning sessions with my Friesian mare, Belle. Belle has worked with many women who have or had breast cancer. She is well aware of the challenges that breast cancer sufferers and survivors have to face, especially their uncertainty about their continued attractiveness and femininity post-mastectomy. She helped Patricia work through these issues. She also helped Patricia increase her self-esteem, by only engaging in activities with Patricia when Patricia approached her with a confident attitude. She pointedly ignored Patricia if she showed any signs of self-doubt. Patricia visualised herself approaching Belle with supreme self-confidence until it became her natural way of approaching anyone and every problem. Belle then started seeking out Patricia's company spontaneously.

"Imagination is more important than knowledge. For while knowledge defines all we currently know and understand, imagination points to all we might yet discover and create. Imagination is everything. It is the preview of life's coming attractions." - Albert Einstein

In the next chapter, we look at a problem that keeps many women from realising their full potential: insomnia.

Chapter 11

Sleep Meditation

Insomaniac's Tweets

Twitter conversation between @insomaniac and @equineguidedmd. 12 September 2015. 03h00.

-I can't sleep.

-@insomaniac, it is 3h00 in the morning!

-Exactly.

-Well, I AM sleeping.

-Lucky you.

-Make yourself some hot chocolate.

-Did that two hours ago.

-Maybe you are hungry. Eat something.

-Ate the rest of the chocolate cake with the hot chocolate.

-Listen to some soothing music?

-#amlistening to Norah Jones' Come away with me. Not working.

-Hot bath?

-Tried it.

-You worried about something?

-Problems at work. Not sleeping = more problems at work.

-Bummer. You tried sleep meditation?

-Sleep meditation?

-Sleep Meditation is a meditation method that can help you sleep better.

Assessing Insomaniac's problem

Isabelle, also known as Insomaniac, not only has difficulty falling asleep but she also often wakes up during the night and then has trouble going back to sleep. Sometimes she wakes up in the early hours of the morning. Not surprisingly, during the day she feels tired and has difficulty concentrating. Her memory lets her down and she is irritable with her colleagues and her family. She has been struggling with insomnia for most of her life. It started in her teens. At the age of 64, it can now definitely be termed a chronic condition. There are periods when she sleeps a bit better and then something happens that starts the infernal cycle again.

She decided to join us for a 5-day mindfulness meditation workshop because the only time she doesn't have any problems falling asleep is when she tries to meditate!

The first night here, contrary to 99% of our guests who mostly sleep deeply and often for twice as long as they normally sleep, Isabelle could not sleep. When we talked about it, it seemed as if Isabelle's chronic insomnia may be related to chronic anxiety.

Helping Isabelle meant first excluding medical causes like nasal allergies, gastrointestinal reflux, hyperthyroidism, arthritis, asthma, chronic pain, sleep apnoea and depression. I checked that she wasn't taking any medications such common cold and nasal allergies remedies, high blood pressure, heart disease or thyroid disease medication that can cause insomnia. Isabelle was already aware that she should not drink coffee close to bedtime. In fact, caffeine can stay in your system for as long as eight hours, so the effects can be long-lasting. Alcohol is not a good idea either, as though it is a sedative, it can make you fall asleep initially, but may disrupt your sleep later in the night. Heavy meals close to bedtime can also disrupt your sleep. It is best to eat a light meal in the evening.

Isabelle often worked late into the night on her laptop. I explained that this can make it harder for her to unwind and it can make you feel preoccupied and anxious when she wants to fall asleep. I also warned that the light from her computer could also make her brain more alert, making it difficult for her to go to sleep. Isabelle's VAK test showed a strong preference for auditory learning with a secondary preference for learning by reading and writing. So, to help her with her insomnia, I suggested that she listens to a recording or that she uses an app.

To understand why she has problems sleeping, we decided to investigate by looking for answers to the following questions:
1. What is Insomnia?
2. Determining the exact nature of your insomnia
3. How to improve your Sleep Pattern

1. What is Insomnia?

Insomnia is defined as the inability to fall asleep or stay asleep for long enough to wake up feeling refreshed the next morning. This happens even though one has had enough time and opportunity to sleep. As mentioned above, symptoms include difficulty falling asleep, frequently waking up during the night, waking up in the early morning hours, sleepiness during the daytime, difficulty concentrating, irritability and still feeling tired after a "full" night's sleep. Anyone can get insomnia, but it is generally more common in women than in men. The elderly is particularly at risk of getting insomnia. Sleeplessness can also be caused by stress and anxiety. Stress/anxiety is one of the most common causes of insomnia.

If you suffer from insomnia, you are not alone. Chronic insomnia affects approximately 30% of the general population. Insomnia affects people from all walks of life, temporarily or permanently, and for a large variety of reasons. It can be acute - when it starts suddenly and persists for a few nights to a couple of weeks, or it can be chronic, when it lasts for months, sometimes for years, as in Isabelle's case.

The reasons we can't sleep at night are usually the same reasons we don't truly live during the day. ~Michael Xavier

2. Determining the exact nature of your insomnia

I suggested to Isabelle that if she wants to find out exactly why she can't sleep, she may find it useful to keep a "sleep diary." Same goes for you, if you suffer from insomnia. It will help you to gain a better understanding of your current sleep pattern. It can also help you decide which method of treatment to use. Most experts ask patients to keep a sleep diary for a minimum of two weeks. The following information should be recorded in your sleep diary:
  · the time that you go bed every night,
  · how long it takes you to fall to sleep,
  · the number of times you wake up during the night,
  · what time it is when you get up,
  · feeling tired during the day,
  · naps you need to take during the day,
  · when and what you eat, when and how much you drink (specifically alcohol and caffeine),
  · when, where and how much you exercise,
  · when and why you are stressed.

Once you have kept your sleep diary for 2 weeks, a pattern will emerge. Now is the time to see your doctor, to exclude any medical causes. He/she will explain that although insomnia may respond to medication, often all you need to do is to improve your sleep hygiene. Your doctor might also suggest a relaxation exercise, like sleep meditation. Sleeping tablets are the last resort. They are mostly only used for short periods and doctors tend to prescribe the lowest possible dose.

3. How to improve your Sleep Pattern
   1. Lifestyle Choices
   2. Mindful Sleep Meditation

a. Lifestyle Choices

Sleep hygiene involves all the things you do, not just before you go to sleep, but during the whole day, that might affect your ability to sleep at night. The following suggestions can help you improve your sleep hygiene:

Go to bed at the same time every night and get up at the same time every morning. During the week but also on weekends and while on vacation.

Use your bed for sleeping in only, not for reading, watching television, surfing the net or working.

Avoid naps, especially in the late afternoon or evening. Avoid falling asleep in front of the TV.

Do not exercise close to bedtime, unless you are doing a sleep-inducing yoga routine.

Take a hot bath about an hour before bedtime.

Buy a comfortable mattress and turn it regularly. The right pillow, for you, is important too.

Do something relaxing in the 30 minutes before bedtime like reading (although not in bed) or go for a leisurely walk.

Make sure your bedroom is neither too hot nor too cold and well-ventilated.

Have a hot drink (not coffee!) or eat something light just before bedtime. This can help you sleep better, although a large meal may have the opposite effect. Chamomile or Valerian tea can help you relax. One cup will do, too many fluids last thing at night will necessitate several trips to the bathroom. During the day, eat food with a high magnesium content, like almonds, cashews, and spinach, as well as food containing a lot of B vitamins, like leafy green vegetables and legumes.

Avoid nicotine, a stimulant, at bedtime. Smokers often have problems sleeping.

Spend some time every day in natural daylight. Half an hour to an hour a day will already make you sleep better.

Schedule "worry time." Decide that you are going to do all your worrying from, say, 18h00 to 18h30 (not too close to bedtime). Do not allow yourself to worry at other times.

The list is not exclusive, it is a matter of finding, by trial and error, what works best for you.

b. Mindful Sleep Meditation

To develop healthier sleep habits, you can use a relaxation exercise like sleep meditation. A recent study, which appeared in the JAMA Internal Medicine, suggests that mindfulness meditation can help insomniacs (see Bibliography).

The study included 49 middle-aged and older adults who had trouble sleeping. Half of the group completed six sessions of a mindfulness-awareness program. They learnt how to meditate and did exercises designed to help them be "present-in-the-moment." The other half of the group took part in a sleep education workshop. They learnt how to improve their sleep hygiene. Compared with the people in the sleep education group, those in the mindfulness group had less insomnia, fatigue and depression at the end of the six sessions.

In 2014, researchers reported on an eight-week trial involving 54 adults with chronic insomnia. People taking part underwent Mindfulness-based Stress Reduction, Mindfulness-based Therapy for Insomnia, or a self-monitoring regime. The researchers found that both of the mindfulness programs were more effective than the self-monitoring routine. They concluded that mindfulness meditation appears to be a viable treatment option for adults with chronic insomnia and could provide an alternative to traditional treatments for insomnia.

Mindfulness meditation involves focusing your attention on the present moment, rather than worrying about what happened in the past or what is going to happen in the future. If your insomnia is caused by stress, and it often is, mindfulness meditation can help you calm your mind down. When we are stressed, a thousand-and-one thoughts rattle around in our minds. Mindfulness meditation helps you focus on the here-and-now. It helps you distance yourself from those thoughts about the past and about the future that are keeping you awake. It helps you relax and because it helps you relax, it can help you sleep better. It can help you fall asleep and stay asleep until you wake up rested and refreshed. Mindfulness is about observing your thoughts one at a time, non-judgmentally, without getting involved with that specific thought before moving on to the next thought. Beginners often find this difficult, but those who persevere end up sleeping much better.

Practising mindfulness meditation during the daytime, learning how to observe your thoughts without getting involved with them, will make it easier to calm your mind down at night. Try regularly practising mindfulness meditation. Not only will it help you sleep better, but it will also help you manage stress better.

Equine-guided Mindfulness Meditation

Did you know that horses can sleep standing up? Indeed, they have a special mechanism in their knees, enabling them to lock their knees in the standing position so that they can sleep standing up. They often do, you will see them stealing a few moments here and there to take a standing nap. They also sleep lying down, but only when they feel completely safe. One of them is often left standing guard, in case a fire-breathing dragon decides to attack the herd.

Wouldn't it have been convenient if people could do the same? A quick nap while standing in a queue could come in useful if you have not slept much the previous night. You may not have slept well because you were out till late. Or, like many of us, you may simply suffer from insomnia: you lie in bed, wide-awake, staring at the ceiling wide-eyed and unable to fall asleep no matter how hard you try...

Most horse people get nervous when they see horses lying down in their field, as it can be a sign that there is something wrong, that the horse is ill. Leo, my little palomino rescue, went down in his field like this 3 days before he died. When I see our horses all lying down, I cannot help but feel anxious. Every time it happens, I rush out into the field and check them, one by one, to make sure nobody feels unwell. When I am sure that they are all just resting, I sit down with Belle, with my back against her back, and listen to her breathing. There is nothing in my world more calming than sitting on the ground in the presence of the herd while they are resting like this. An overwhelming sense of peace comes over me and soon my eyes close...sometimes I meditate, sometimes I fall asleep.

Isabelle's Meditation Method: Body Scan Meditation

One way to induce sleep by mindfully meditating is by doing a body scan meditation. When you are feeling stressed and anxious, it is common to focus the feeling in one or another body part: a thunderous frown, a clenched jaw, scrunched-up shoulders, balled fists, tummy doing flip-flops, tightly curled toes...A body scan meditation can be performed daily or even several times a day, as needed, to help you identify what you are feeling, where you're feeling it and to help you release the stress in your body...and also in your mind.

Body scan meditation is one of the meditation techniques taught by MBSR (Mindfulness-Based Stress Reduction, developed by Prof Jon Kabat-Zinn) instructors like Trish Magyari, who explain that the purpose of the body scan is "to bring awareness to each part of our body sequentially, to see how it is today — not to change or judge the body, which we are often so quick to do, but just to experience it and see what's there." The purpose of this body scan mindfulness meditation is simply to notice your body, simply being aware of your body, in this present moment.

According to Prof Jon Kabat-Zinn, "In the body scan, we are developing greater intimacy with bare sensation, opening to the give-and-take embedded in the reciprocity between the sensations themselves and our awareness of them. As a result, it is not uncommon to be less disturbed by them, or disturbed by them in a different, a wiser way, even when they are acute. Awareness learns to let them be as they are and to hold them without triggering so much emotional reactivity and also so much inflamed thinking about them. We sometimes speak of awareness and discernment differentiating and perhaps naturally "uncoupling" the sensory dimension of the experience of pain from the emotional and cognitive dimensions of pain. In the process, the intensity of the sensations themselves can sometimes subside. In any event, they may come to be seen as less onerous, less debilitating."

Usually, our response to bodily pain or discomfort is to distract ourselves or to try and numb/ignore the pain. In this exercise, we notice with patient curiosity if our bodies are comfortable or uncomfortable. The body scan cultivates our ability to be present in our bodies, in the moment, exploring the experience with curiosity and receptiveness, breathing quietly during discomfort and examining our discomfort instead of avoiding it/suppressing it.

One could start with one's feet, paying attention to the physical feelings in them: pain, discomfort, coolness, warmth, tension or tightness. Simply pay attention to the physical sensations.

"Usually, when people find something in their body they don't like, they meet it with judgement; the body that's in pain is your enemy," Magyari says. "It's a very radical concept to meet the body with friendliness."

You then take a tour of your body – mentally – by noticing and experiencing each part. Once a part is scanned, one allows awareness of that part to fade away as we move to the next area. Slowly allow your awareness to drift up from your feet to your lower legs, again simply paying attention to any physical sensations in that part of your body. Let your awareness drift further up your body – to your thighs, hips, buttocks, pelvic region, belly, chest, your lower back, upper back, fingers and hands, lower arms, upper arms, shoulders, neck, your head, forehead, temples, face – eyes, cheeks, nose, mouth, jaw.

This whole process can take from 5 short minutes to 30 minutes. You can body scan in as little as 5 minutes, although it is said that the most benefits are achieved during longer body scans. Body scanning trains your mind and narrows your focus moving from one body part to the next and ultimately your body as a whole. Each time your mind drifts, notice what it was focusing on without judgement and bring your attention back to your breathing. At the end of the exercise, as you breathe in, imagine your in-breath starting at your toes and reaching the top of your head. As you breathe out, your out-breath sweeps from the top of your head down to your toes.

"At the very end, we're lying with the awareness of our wholeness in that moment. We're not thinking about what's right or wrong with us, our state of health, but just that sense of physical wholeness," Magyari says.

According to MBSRtraining.com, bringing mindfulness to the body can help you learn what your body does and does not need in order to thrive. "The body scan meditation is a deep investigation into the moment-to-moment experiences of the body. By bringing awareness and acknowledgement to whatever you feel or sense in the body, the body scan can be very helpful in working with stress, anxiety and physical pain."

Prof Kabat-Zinn says, "The body scan is not for everybody, and it is not always the meditation of choice even for those who love it. But it is extremely useful and good to know about and practice from time to time, whatever your circumstances or condition. If you think of your body as a musical instrument, the body scan is a way of tuning it. If you think of it as a universe, the body scan is a way to come to know it. If you think of your body as a house, the body scan is a way to throw open all the windows and let the fresh air of awareness sweep it clean."

I suggested the Body Scan Meditation on YouTube recorded by Prof Kabat-Zinn to Isabelle.

Using an App

Alternatively, I suggested to Isabelle that she might benefit from doing a guided sleep meditation. There is a huge variety of these available on YouTube, lasting from ten minutes to eight hours. Or she could use a Sleep Meditation App like "Sleepeasy." The Sleepeasy app contains a wide variety of guided meditations to help you fall asleep and stay deeply asleep. You can listen to the meditations with or without music/nature sounds. In addition, you can create your own sleep program using a Playlist feature which allows you to listen to up to six meditations in one session.

There are, in fact, numerous mindfulness Apps that can help you sleep better. Most of them have a free introduction series of sessions. Some then ask you to subscribe for a small monthly fee should you wish to continue. Another favourite is "Calm. "Calm" won a best App award in 2017. The initial 7-day series on sleep, when followed in sequence, provides a good grounding in mindfulness.

Using a Recording

I often encourage our workshop participants to try a relaxing, sleep-inducing guided meditation on their first night here with us. They often arrive here on the farm still stressed by their journey. Their minds are often still busy with the problems they left behind at work and at home. A guided sleep meditation helps them to fall asleep and stay asleep till breakfast the next morning. I have made a playlist of the best guided meditations currently available on YouTube, so each of our guests can choose the meditation that appeals to them most.

When you listen to a guided sleep meditation, you are more or less hypnotising yourself. Charles Dickens refers to this state, that we often go through just before we finally fall asleep, "There is a drowsy state, between sleeping and waking, when you dream more in five minutes with your eyes half open, and yourself half conscious of everything that is passing around you, than you would in five nights with your eyes fast closed and your senses wrapped in perfect unconsciousness."

For easy access, I have collected a couple of guided "falling asleep" meditations in a playlist on YouTube. It is worth listening to one of these recordings with earphones on. Listening to a recording is deeply relaxing, nearly as good as sleeping itself. If your mind drifts off, onto other subjects, don't worry about it, it's normal, just always bring your thoughts back to the recording. There are loads of these recordings on YouTube, of various lengths, some better than others.

Or you can access my playlist on YouTube at my channel called Margaretha Montagu. My favourite sleep meditation is the last one on the list. In the next chapter, one of my favourite subjects: Gratitude and its extensive benefits.

Chapter 12

Equine-guided Mindfulness Meditation

Lucinda's Letter

"Dear Margaretha Montagu,

I understand that you run mindfulness meditation workshops that include equine-guided meditation. I am interested to find out more about this meditation method. I am also interested in equine-assisted experiential learning. I think it could help me.

Since I first met one at the age of six, horses have always fascinated me. One of my earliest memories. I never had the opportunity to ride, but horses have nevertheless directly or indirectly played an important role in my life. I am a writer. I write young adult fiction and most of my books feature one or more horses.

I am writing to you today because I have an acute case of writer's block that is threatening to become chronic. I have not been able to write a publishable word since October last year. Seven months ago. My writing is my livelihood. I usually have no trouble writing a novel a year. I have had writer's block before, but always in the past, it disappeared again within a couple of days. Now, my inability to write has become a real problem. In fact, it was as I was researching "writer's block" that I found your Walking And Wine Tasting Weekends advert. A walking and wine tasting weekend sounds like just the thing I need! I have always wanted to walk the Santiago de Compostelle pilgrim's route. Incredible to think that this route is nearly a thousand years old. Following in the footsteps of hundreds of thousands of pilgrims who have walked the path must be an unforgettable experience. I can well understand that it could help with writer's block. I know of several now-famous authors who started writing after walking the Camino. I know of several who were inspired by their walk to write a book detailing their adventures. I have read just about every book on the subject. I particularly enjoyed Paulo Coelho's "The Pilgrimage," Katharine Elliott's "A Camino of the Soul: Learning to Listen When the Universe Whispers" and Shirley MacClain's "The Camino: A Journey of the Spirit." Walking the whole route will never be an option, but walking it for two days would be heaven.

I wondered if I could combine the two options? Could I do the mindfulness meditation workshop during the week and the walking and writing workshop over the weekend? I understand that you do exceptionally host private workshops. At this moment in time, I am definitely in need of a custom-made workshop. It is not that I do not enjoy other people's company, on the contrary. The problem is that writer's block is not my only affliction, I am also visually handicapped. I am not completely blind. I have about 20% of vision left in one eye. Usually, I can find my way around, but during the workshop, I will need some help. I will not be able to walk the Camino on my own.

This is why I am also interested in equine-assisted experiential learning. I have not always been partially sighted. I started losing my sight about three years ago. Although I have had lots of help to enable me to remain as independent as possible, my self-confidence has taken a severe blow. Having read your French Confidence made Simple book, I know that you will understand exactly what I mean. I would like to work with you and with the horses to rebuild my self-esteem. I have read quite a bit about equine-assisted experiential learning. I understand that equine-assisted experiential learning is a result-focused approach to personal development that enables you to develop more successful problem-solving skills, communicate more effectively, build healthier relationships and significantly increase your self-confidence. I know I will benefit from it. I found the videos and descriptions on your equine-assisted learning web page very useful. These helped me to understand how the process actually works.

My inability to write is causing my stress levels to rise. That is why I am also interested in equine-guided meditation. Although I am a meditation newbie, I am familiar with mindfulness. My eye problems have made me much more aware of the need to live in the moment. I have learnt to appreciate every sighted second that I have left. Since I write about horses a lot, I am hoping that being constantly in their presence will inspire me. Most of the horses in my books have been Friesians, but I have never before had the opportunity to meet one in person.

If possible, I would like to book a private workshop. It would be helpful if the week could be extended to two weeks if we both think I need to stay longer.

Kind Regards,
  Lucinda Meyer."

My reply to this letter was short and to the point: "No problem. Just let me know when it suits you to come here," because I believe that horses can make people feel better. I know, from personal experience, that when you feel low or anxious, being in the presence of horses - watching horses, talking to them, touching them, walking with them, sitting with them and breathing with them - can make you feel happier and less worried. I have found out that the effect is magnified when you are fully present in the moment, when you stop regretting what happened in the past or worrying what might happen in the future, when you observe the thoughts that pop into your head without interacting with them. This is what I understand mindfulness meditation to be and that is why equine-guided mindfulness meditation is part of my workshops.

I also believe that horses can help us develop and implement better coping strategies. In this, I am not alone. Over the last 10 years, equine-assisted experiential learning (EEL), as an aid to personal and professional development, has become an established discipline. I have seen, first hand, how EEL changes our workshop participants' lives.

I did not have to do an assessment of Lucinda's problem as her letter made it quite clear. It was also obvious that her preferred VAK interpretation mode was the reading/writing one. I already know that writers find walking the Camino inspirational and I thought that she would definitely benefit from equine-guided meditation as well as equine-assisted personal development. As her VAK preference is reading/writing, I suggested that keeping a gratitude diary as a mindful gratitude meditation might work well for her.

First, she had a few questions:
1. What is Equine-guided Mindfulness Meditation?
2. What happens during an Equine-guided Meditation session?
3. What is Equine-assisted Personal Development? (see EquineGuidedGrowth.com)
4. How does Gratitude Meditation work?
5. What are the benefits of Gratitude Meditation?
6. How does one "do" Gratitude Meditation?

1. What is Equine-guided Mindfulness Meditation?

Equine-guided Meditation is a meditation method that is practised in the presence of one or more horses. Equine-guided Meditation is a mindfulness meditation method – it helps you to train your brain to concentrate, to focus your attention on the present and dismiss any distractions that come along. One of my favourite mindfulness authors, Prof Jon Kabat-Zinn, defines mindfulness as "paying attention on purpose, in the present moment, and non-judgmentally, to the unfolding of experience moment to moment." Horses can make it easier for us to do this.

Mindfulness meditation with horses can enable you to:
- enrich your relationships,
- process your emotions more effectively and increase your emotional stability,
- increase your ability to concentrate,
- reduce your vulnerability to distress,
- sleep better and
- increase your overall productivity and creativity.

Initially, when I started sharing this practice with our workshop participants, I called it equine-facilitated meditation. My intention was that it would be focused meditation, with the horse serving as the focus point. My idea was that the horse or horses would facilitate meditation in a passive way.

2. What happens during an Equine-guided Meditation session?

I usually start an equine-facilitated meditation by directing participants to a peaceful spot somewhere near the horses where we can all sit down in a circle. To help our workshop participants reach that state of thoughtless yet alert awareness that I understand meditation to be, I begin by asking them to concentrate on their breathing. At first, we breathe normally. We then gradually let our breathing slow down until it is regular, smooth and slow. If this seems hard at first, I suggest that participants count their breaths. This simple technique involves counting 1, as you breathe in. As you breathe out, count 1 again. Breathe in, count 2. Breathe out, count 2. Count to 10, then count backwards to 1 again. The counting connects your mind to your breath. If you lose count, simply return to 1 and start over.

I then ask participants to focus their attention on one of our horses. I encourage them to engage all five their senses. I ask them to imagine that they are a horse, that they can see, hear, smell, feel and even taste what a horse sees, hears, smells, feels and tastes. I suggest that they imagine how it would feel to have four legs, four hooves and a tail. I ask them to imagine moving like a horse: walking, trotting, cantering, rolling and rearing.

Next, I encourage them to look at their problems as a horse would look at a problem. Horses handle problems as members of a herd, interdependently.

I soon added mindfulness to our equine-facilitated meditations. Prof Jon Kabat-Zinn says, "Mindfulness means maintaining a moment-by-moment awareness of our thoughts, feelings, sensations and surroundings." I explain to participants, that if any distracting thoughts should interfere, they should notice these in a non-judgemental way. They should then allow the thoughts to fade away again.

Guests are often surprised to find that when they are sitting in the paddock with the horses, it is much easier to quieten their minds and enter the meditative state than it is at home. Especially if they do not have much experience with meditation. Horses' ability to be at once fully present in their bodies, in their environment as well as in the moment, facilitates mindful meditation by giving us a perfect example to follow and to focus on. Our workshop participants often continue to practice equine-facilitated meditation at home, by imagining that they were still in the paddock with the horses or by watching YouTube videos.

It worked quite well, until the day I decided to add a loving-kindness meditation at the end of a session. That day, everything changed. We were a small group, no more than six. We were sitting in a circle in the paddock closest to the lake. Belle, Bass, Aurore and Tess were with us in the paddock, grazing peacefully nearby. I lead the loving-kindness meditation, starting with the focus on each of us personally: "May I be filled with loving-kindness. May I feel connected, calm and contented. May I accept myself just as I am. May I be happy…"

I then moved the focus to someone each participant loved. "May you be filled with loving-kindness. May you feel connected, calm and contented. May you accept yourself just as you are, etc. "Next, I moved the focus to the horses. I asked the participants to send waves of loving-kindness to Belle, our boss mare. Before I had voiced the second sentence, Belle had walked over to us and was standing just outside the circle. She had never approached a circle before. It was intimidating because we were sitting flat on the ground and Belle is an enormous horse. As I started the third sentence, she came over to me and made it quite clear that she intended entering the circle. I moved slightly to the side, out of the way of those dinner-plate-sized hooves. Unperturbed, she took her place at the centre of the circle. We all sat there staring at her with our eyes wide, not sure what was going to happen next.

As I moved on the next phrase, Belle went into equine relaxation mode. She started licking and chewing. She sighed, slowed and deepened her breathing. She yawned and lowered her head. She stood like this for a few moments. As I continued with the loving-kindness meditation, moving the focus to the circle, the community and the country, Belle did the rounds. She went up to each person in turn. Sometimes she just stood close. Sometimes she breathed on someone's hair. Sometimes she rested her head for a moment on theirs. We were so engrossed in what was happening, that we had not noticed that the other three horses had approached too. They were now standing just behind us. Aurore and Tess were standing together, and Bass slightly apart. When she had ministered to everyone, Belle left the circle and walked off, the other three following in her wake.

The group was so high after that experience that it took them three days before they came back down to earth. It was clear that something had happened to each of them. I asked each one in turn what the experience had meant to her. The answers varied but they all mentioned an inner awareness of contentedness and sometimes a deeply-moving sense of connection and understanding. That day, our equine-facilitated meditations became equine-guided meditations.

For those of you who love horses and who would love to spend some time in their presence but cannot do so, for whatever reason, at this moment in time, I have created the equine-guided mindfulness meditation online course (EMMOC.) You can access it at my website EquineGuidedGrowth.com

Many great horsemen and horsewomen have noticed this uncanny ability of horses to connect with people. Charles de Kunffy sums up the benefits of spending time with horses as follows: "Horses forge the mind, the character, the emotions and inner lives of humans. People can talk to one another about all these things and remain distanced and lonesome. In partnership with a horse, one is seldom lacking for thought, emotion and inspiration. One is always attended by a great companion."

I first came across equine-facilitated meditation while I was looking for ways to improve my relationship with Belle de la Babinière, my soul mare. I agree with Dominique Barbier when he says, "The only limits I have found have been my own. Where our own egos regularly allow fear and negativity to interfere with our ability to let go and form spiritual connections, horses possess an incalculable ability to function as conduits of connection," and "Where we analyse, where we try to explain, where we try to re-create, where we try to simply be, horses are already there – waiting for us to walk through the open door, to follow the path of spiritual oneness, to allow healing energy to come in."

Lucinda's Meditation Method: Gratitude Meditation

4. How does Gratitude Meditation work?

I am infinitely grateful that I discovered equine-guided mindfulness meditation. I therefore cannot write a book about mindfulness and meditation without mentioning gratitude. I was tempted, though, because I intend to write a whole book about gratefulness, so I initially thought that I would leave the subject out of this one. I could not. Equine-guided meditation, the opportunity to share it with others and the life-changing effect it often has on our workshop participants' lives, fills me with gratitude, time and again. In the end, I decided that I have to at least mention gratitude meditation, and what better place to do so than in the chapter about equine-guided mindfulness meditation. When I practice equine-guided mindfulness meditation, an overwhelming feeling of gratitude often overcomes me. Once I have quieted my mind, with the assistance of the horses, once I am able to non-judgmentally observe my thoughts floating by, in that quiet, peaceful moment, gratitude often happens. Often.

I believe in the magic of gratitude.

I believe the more I feel grateful, the more I have to feel grateful about.

I believe that gratitude is an active process: It is as much about giving as it is about receiving. My understanding of gratitude is that gratitude is not only about being thankful. It is also about appreciating and about repaying kindnesses. In other words, the more you get, the more you give.

This is where the expression, the "gratitude attitude," comes from. People with an attitude of gratitude make time every day to express their gratitude. They either remind themselves how grateful they are or they talk about it to others. Some people write about it in gratitude diaries. Grateful people are mindful, throughout the day, of events or experiences that they are thankful for.

Everyone can do it. Anytime, anywhere. Right now. Just for a moment, be mindful of what you are grateful for. I am hugely grateful that I have a computer and that I have access to the Internet. I am thankful that I can, by touching a few buttons, communicate with people thousands of kilometres away. I am grateful that my desk faces a window and that I can see three of our horses peacefully grazing. I can also see one that is attempting to reach a blade of grass on the other side of the fence by doing a downward dog yoga pose. I am thankful that I have a glass of pure spring water by my side, as well as a bowl of Mirabelle plums from our own tree. Just at this moment, I cannot think of anything else I could possibly need, or anywhere else I would rather be.

Gratitude is about appreciating the moment. Mindfully.

5. What are the benefits of Gratitude Meditation?

But what good is gratitude in the long run?

Well, it makes me feel good. Happy. More confident. It enriches my relationships. It makes me feel more positive about the future, which makes me sleep better. It makes me feel more satisfied with my life, and with life in general.

Gratitude can also help us manage stress better. Robert Emmons, a psychology professor at the University of California at Davis, has conducted research showing that those who make time to be grateful manage stress much better than those who do not. The connection between gratitude and stress management is not immediately obvious. How will making a list of the things that I am thankful for help me to cope with stress? This is how it works: Gratitude allows you to look at stress from a different perspective. It helps you to focus on positive experiences and emotions rather than negative ones. Realising how much you have to be grateful for can increase your self-esteem and your self-confidence. If you appreciate the people who care for you and who support you, you will feel better equipped to cope with stressful situations. Gratitude also inspires generosity. Giving to others, whether they in return are grateful or not, increases your general sense of well-being. Gratitude makes you want to "pay it forward."

Prof Emmons' findings, along with those from other researchers such as Lisa Aspinwall, a psychology professor at the University of Utah, suggest that grateful people may be more likely to:

- take care of themselves physically and mentally,
- get regular exercise,
- eat a healthy diet,
- are more alert and attentive,
- cope more effectively with challenges,
- feel happier and more optimistic,
- have stronger immune systems,
- maintain a positive view of the future.

Clearly, it would be a good idea to incorporate gratitude into your meditation practice.

6. But how does one "do" Gratitude Meditation?

- As I mentioned, you can keep a gratitude diary. I thought this would work well for Lucinda. All you have to do, is to write down five things that you are thankful for every day. You then meditate on these five things. You are mindful of them, as you go through your day. There are many custom-made gratitude journals to choose from. One of my favourites is "The Simple Abundance Journal of Gratitude" by Sarah Ban Breathnach. This diary is a companion to Sarah's book "Simple Abundance." This beautiful journal provides a place to record the five things that you are grateful or every day. It provides inspiration with gratitude quotes. If you would like to use quotes for inspiration, you will find a collection of uplifting gratitude quotes on Pinterest at Margaretha's Muse. If you find the quotes inspiring, please follow me on Pinterest - I save everything that inspires me on there: quotes, articles, blog posts, recipes, French Country decorating ideas etc.

- Or you can join the "Gratitude Project" at Thnx4.org where you can register for a 10-day Intensive Gratitude Challenge either individually or as part of a group. Thnx4.org also introduces its users to a guided, two-week exercise designed by experts to help people make gratitude a daily practice. Every day, users get tips on how to be grateful. Users are able to keep a private journal and say "thanx" publicly on Facebook, Twitter, WhatsApp etc. Users of the site can also read expressions of gratitude from other people in the community. In the end, users discover how 14 days of gratitude awareness affected their mood and health.

- As I mentioned in the chapter about writing meditation, we do gratitude meditations during our workshops by reflecting on questions such as: "What have I received from ...?" and "What have I given to ...?" You can do the same, every morning and every evening. In the mornings you could ask yourself: "What am I grateful for this morning? What can I do to help someone else today?" In the evening you could ask yourself, "What happened today that I am grateful for? What have I done today to make someone else's life easier?" I wrote a blog post some time ago about Paying it forward. It is about a courageous group of women who save several horses from drowning.

There is always something to be grateful for.

"There are many things for which we cannot be grateful, but there is no moment for which we cannot be grateful, because in every moment, even difficult ones, we have the opportunity to do something." — David Steindl-Rast

- You can say a prayer of gratitude (see chapter 9). In many spiritual traditions, prayers of gratitude are considered to be the most powerful form of prayer. It does not have to be a long or complicated statement. You can simply say "Thank you." You can use "Thank You" as your prayer word during contemplative meditation.

- You could read a script or watch a YouTube guided meditation. You will find several gratitude meditation scripts online. Just do a "gratitude meditation" and "script" search. There are several guided gratitude meditations on YouTube.

- You can visit David Steindl-Rast's website gratefulness.org. This is an interactive website with several thousand participants from more than 240 countries. You can light a virtual candle here as a mindfulness, serenity and solidarity exercise. "It is the integral practice of grateful living," says Brother David, "that unites Christianity, Buddhism and all other religious traditions." You can also send a Thank you e-card from this site.

I once saw a mind-altering TED talk by David Steindl-Rast, "an inspiring lesson in slowing down, looking where you're going, and above all, about being grateful." David is a Benedictine monk. He has a PhD in experimental psychology. He was a post-Doctoral Fellow at Cornell University, where he also held the Thorpe Lectureship. He was one of the first Roman Catholics to participate in Buddhist-Christian dialogue. David is the author of "The Ground we share" – a text on Buddhist and Christian practice, written with Robert Aitken Roshi. He is also the author of "99 blessings."

I would like to invite you to make gratitude part of your meditation practice, whichever meditation methods you choose to practice. During working meditation practice, you can choose to be thankful that you are strong enough to work, that you are skilled enough, or that you can work inside or outside. During walking meditation, you can feel grateful that you have two working legs, that you were able to make time to go for a walk or that it isn't raining. During a writing meditation, you can feel grateful, like me, that you can do your writing on a computer, that your eyes can see well enough for you to write or that you have finally found the perfect diary to write in. During a music meditation...well, where shall I start? You can be grateful that you can hear. You can feel thankful that your choice of music is available at the touch of a button or you can feel grateful towards the composers of your favourite music... Every meditation method can inspire you to feel thankful. Even sitting meditation can inspire gratitude. You could remind yourself that you can breathe easily and painlessly - something many thousands of asthma and emphysema sufferers would be only too grateful for.

Gratitude is an integral part of our mindfulness meditation workshops.

It is gratitude that inspired us to start sharing this beautiful patch of paradise with other people. Contact and connection with horses, especially when during meditation, can teach us the skills we need to handle the trials and turbulence of life: perseverance, patience, self-discipline, empathy, forgiveness, leadership and much more. If you would like to experience this unique meditation method, you are welcome to join us for a few days to a Connect with Horses mindfulness and meditation workshop here in the south of France. Simply send an e-mail to welcome2gascony@gmail.com asking for more information. Making an enquiry puts you under no obligation. More about this in the next chapter.

"Dedicating some time to meditation is a meaningful expression of caring for yourself that can help you move through the mire of feeling unworthy. As your mind grows quieter and more spacious, you can begin to see self-defeating thought patterns for what they are, and open up to other, more positive options."
  Sharon Salzberg

Personal Empowerment Workshops

Connect with Horses Workshops

Based on Mindfulness and Meditation

My Twitter profile says I am a "recycled MD, a writer and mindfulness and meditation workshop presenter." In a nutshell, that is about right. You already know that I am a writer. In addition to this book, you may also have read French Women's Confidence Secrets. If not, you can read the second chapter at the end of this book. I also present Connect with Horses mindfulness and meditation workshops. You may have noticed a couple of not-so-subtle references to my workshops in this book. You may have wondered what it is all about, especially Equine-assisted Experiential Learning (EEL). Did I mention EEL? I am sure I did. I must have. Several times. You may even, in desperation, have clicked on an EEL link and you may now know exactly what EEL is.

The reason I mention the workshops so often is because one of the best ways to find the right meditation method for you is to try out the different methods, with guidance, until you find one that fits. That is certainly true about equine guided meditation. The best way to see if it will work for you is to try it out in person, in the presence of horses. (For those of you who love horses and who would love to spend some time in their presence but cannot do so, for whatever reason, at this moment in time, I have created the equine-guided mindfulness meditation online course (EMMOC.) You can access it at my website EquineGuidedGrowth.com) Hosting the workshops is one of my favourite activities of all times, so I would much rather show you how it works, in person.

As you have seen, each of the chapters in this book starts with an e-mail, a text or a telephone call that I received from a potential workshop participant. I couldn't very well NOT mention the workshops. If these rather too frequently-occurring references are starting to get on your nerves, I apologise. I will stop doing it immediately. I will make everything clear right away. At the end of this chapter, you will know everything you ever wanted to know about my Connect with Horses workshops.

I initially created these workshops because I am obsessed with helping people manage stress more effectively. Mindfulness and meditation can help you deal more effectively with stress. It can help you avoid the physical and mental damage that stress can cause. That is why I set out to write this book, to help people manage stress with mindfulness and meditation. It was just going to be a standard "Find the right meditation method for you" book. As you may have gathered, my horses had other ideas.

"Thanks again for sharing your life with us! I had such a wonderful time at your place and in your company. I feel revitalised, relaxed and blessed. All the best and big hugs for the two of you and all the cats, horses and dog." E.G. Meijling

"A powerful and wonderful life experience, with caring guidance. One can truly experience a mindful meditation with the horses who are definitely spiritual. Also, your senses become reinvigorated with the beautiful food and wine, whilst sitting and listening to the unique sound of nature's calmness." S. Murphy

Why would you want to attend a Connect with Horses Personal Development workshop?

Right, this chapter is supposed to be about my workshops. So, the idea of the workshops is to offer participants the chance to get away from the challenges and demands of everyday life. When you attend one of my workshops here in the south of France, you will have time to rest, to reflect and to recharge your batteries. You will be able to leave the complexity of your daily life behind, with all its demands, deadlines, doubts and disagreements. You will be encouraged to:
- put yourself first without feeling guilty,
- discover or re-discover your life's purpose,
- uncover your full potential,
- spend time "being" rather than "doing,"
- de-stress and learn how to manage stress more effectively,
- re-connect with your authentic self,
- look at your life from a distance and from a different perspective,
- eradicate limiting beliefs that hold you back,
- get rid of unhealthy habits,
- make new, like-minded friends,
- exchange your inner critic for an inner cheerleader,
- spend time enjoying the beauty of nature,
- boost your creativity,
- find inspiration and motivation to make permanent changes,
- investigate mindfulness and meditation as effective stress management strategies,
- choose the meditation technique that works best for you
- focus on what is important to you,
- forget about the shopping you need to do, the food you need to cook, the dishes you need to wash,
- experiment with leaving your comfort zone,
- say what you want to say without having to worry about the consequences,

- rebuild your shattered self-image,
- process past experiences,
- count your blessings,
- sleep peacefully and undisturbed for as long as you need to,
- stop making excuses
- and just be YOU.

A substantial number of you will read this book, I hope, will choose a meditation method that works for them and succeed in managing stress much more effectively. A small number of you will find the idea of trying out the various meditation methods while staying in one of the most beautiful parts of France irresistible. Eh bien, you are soooooo very welcome here if you feel the need to get away from all the hustle-and-bustle, not only to rest but also to be able to concentrate fully on what you want to learn. These workshops offer you the opportunity to deepen your awareness of yourself, of other people, of horses and of the world around you. My mindfulness meditation workshops are personal transformational and empowerment workshops that can be challenging and life-changing experiences.

This is where Equine-assisted Experiential Learning comes in.

The aim of my workshops is to enable women (and a few men too along the way) to put the principles described in this book into practice with the help of our horses. These personal empowerment workshops are unique because they offer participants the opportunity to discover equine-assisted experiential learning (EEL) and equine-guided mindfulness.

EEL will help you:
- free yourself from immobilising fear and so dramatically increase your self-confidence,
- discover simple techniques to easily and effectively deal with

stressful situations
- communicate more efficiently and with more assertiveness,
- find out how to accept and appreciate yourself,
- strengthen and deepen relationships at work and at home,
- eradicate limiting beliefs and replace them with empowering beliefs,
- develop more successful problem-solving skills,
- thrive on change and challenges and
- gain a solid understanding of who you are now.
- Having thus substantially increased your self-confidence, you could
- leave your dead-end job and find a much better one,
- ask for that raise you know you deserve,
- start the business you have always dreamed of owning,
- go back to school and get the qualifications you want,
- build solid relationships with your significant other, your parents, your children, your friends and family...

Do you feel over-burdened by the trials and tribulations of life? Do you feel physically exhausted and mentally strangled and desperately long to escape? Would you like to develop more successful problem-solving skills, communicate more effectively, build healthier relationships and significantly increase your self-confidence? If you do, then a Connect with Horses Mindfulness Meditation workshop in the sun-drenched south of France may just be exactly what you need to help you put the principles discussed in this book into practice.

If you are looking for a purely relaxing spa retreat, spending your days detoxing and being pampered, then a Connect with Horses personal empowerment workshop is not for you. If you want to relax and get away from it all, but you also want to take a good look at who you are now and where you want to go from here, then one of our workshops would be a good investment in your personal wellbeing. Our participants attend 3/5/7 or 10-day workshops. To find out more, visit EquineGuidedGrowth.com or e-mail me on at welcome2gascony@gmail.com.

Chapter 20

Conclusion

You will find most of the free downloads and other links mentioned in this book HERE.

We have looked at a selection of meditation methods in this book. I chose to include these specific methods because they offer alternatives to the traditional method of sitting meditation and because most can be enriched by the presence of horses. I chose to write about mindfulness and meditation because so many of my workshop participants say that stress management is what they most need help with. My aim with this book (and with my workshops) is to enable as many people as possible to use these strategies to combat stress and so avoid the possible physical and mental damage that stress can cause. Yes, I know I keep repeating myself, but it is because this is VERY important!

I hope that you have found, between these pages, a meditation method that suits you. I know that starting a meditation practice is easy but keeping it up is more difficult, so I use social media and my blog to continue to inspire and motivate my readers. If you have a question, do not hesitate to contact me via one of these channels:

- Blog: blog with lots of inspirational blog posts about mindfulness, meditation and the south of France. You can subscribe to my blog at my website EquineGuidedGrowth.com

- Twitter: @EquineGuidedMD. I always let my followers know when I have published a new blog post/new book or when I am doing a giveaway. I regularly tweet stress-busting quotes, memes and tips.

- LinkedIn as Margaretha Montagu

- Facebook: Margaretha Montagu's Workshops and Books. I share interesting articles that I come across on the web on my Facebook page. Memes too, I love creating memes.

- Pinterest: Margaretha's Muse Here you can explore my Self-confidence, Self-compassion, Self-talk and Support Systems boards for more stress-busting articles, books, pictures, courses, etc. Most written by experts in the field.

-Medium.com: I write articles on Medium about subjects that do not fit my blog ex. *What is wrong with the Law of Attraction* and *Intermittent Fasting works*, also under my pen name Margaretha Montagu

That is about it, I think. One last thing. I would appreciate it enormously if you would write a review for this book. Just hop over to my Author page at Amazon and click on the book that you want to review.

Legal Disclaimer

This is a work of fiction. The contents are based on the author's personal experience and research. Names, characters, places and incidents are the products of the author's imagination. Although every precaution has been taken to verify the accuracy of the information contained in this book, the author and publisher assume no responsibility for any errors or omissions. There are no representations or warranties, express or implied, about the completeness, accuracy, reliability, suitability or availability with respect to the information, products, services or related graphics contained in this e-book for any purpose. Any use of this information is at your own risk.

The entire content of this e-book is copyrighted. Copyright © Margaretha de Klerk aka Margaretha Montagu. All rights reserved. No part

Medical Disclaimer

Free Preview

Free Preview

Self-Confidence Made Simple
   16 Frenchwomen share their Self-esteem Secrets
   Seven Steps to Sustainable Self-Confidence
   MargarethaMontagu.com
   EquineGuidedGrowth.com
   MargarethaMontagu@gmail.com
   French women are famous for their effortless elegance, their enchanting independence, their irresistible charm and their unshakeable self-confidence.

In my book, Self-Confidence Made Simple: 16 Frenchwomen share their Self-esteem Secrets, a handful of my closest French friends share their confidence secrets with you. I have lived in France for part of my childhood and for most of my adult life. I have spent nearly twenty-five years, first as a medical doctor and more recently as a workshop leader, empowering women to live long, happy, healthy and fulfilling lives, full of purpose and meaning. It's my life's mission.

In this book, you will meet these French women: Anaïs, Inès, Lisa, Marie-Thérèse, Claire, Régine, Amèlie, Corrine, Béatrice, Annie, Monique and Eloïse, who will share their stories with you.

As you share these women's joys and sorrows, you will discover how they remain unconditionally self-confident, serenely sophisticated and perfectly poised no matter how challenging the situations are that they find themselves in. To each story and to every secret, I have added my (by now) extensive knowledge and experience, with practical suggestions to help you incorporate each of these potentially life-changing strategies into your own life.

Self-Confidence Made Simple is a guide to becoming a woman who knows exactly who she is, who takes excellent care of herself, who leads a balanced, purposeful and fulfilling life, who has a solid support network, who can laugh at herself, who knows she has a lot to be grateful for, who knows how to forgive, who competently handles stress, who knows how to say NO without apologising and who knows that being ageless is all about attitude.

If you too want to master the skills you need to develop rock-solid self-confidence, this book is for you. Below you will find an extract from the book, the Contents, Introduction and most of Chapter 2, to give you an idea of how the book is put together and of how it can help you dramatically increase your self-confidence.

Contents

Introduction
  Dedication
  French women are confident:
  · Because they know how to look after themselves - Chapter 1 Sumptuous Self-Care
  · Because they know exactly who they are - Chapter 2 Choosing and Changing Your Identity
  · Because they know how to keep their lives in balance - Chapter 3 Balancing Act
  · Because they have extensive support systems - Chapter 4 Rock-

solid Support Systems
- Because they never forget how much they have to be grateful for – Chapter 5 Gratitude and Generosity
- Because they know how to deal with stress and make it work for them – Chapter 6 Taming and Harnessing Stress
- Because they do not allow resentment to erode their confidence – Chapter 7 Forgiveness
- Implementing the French Approach – Chapter 9

Conclusion

Bibliography

Links to: Self-care Quiz, Self-Confidence Quiz, Self-Criticism Quiz, Stress Quiz, Vision Board Guide, Creative Visualisation Guide

Introduction

I opened the car door and carefully placed my borrowed Louboutins on the tarmac. Tottering over to the sliding doors felt like walking on soft, sticky toffee. The resemblance stopped there. There was no smell of melting sweetness, the city air was thick with pollution. My thin summer dress was sticking to my back. That summer, one heat wave relentlessly succeeded another in the south of France. The south of France is not the paradise it is made out to be. The only reason I left the sanctuary of my ancient farmhouse to come into the city during siesta time was to support my French friend Anais. Anais was taking part in a fashion show. I wished I could leave the Louboutins right there in the middle of the road. I am a horsewoman. As a rule, I am much more comfortable in riding boots. Not so my super-stylish friend Anais. Anais is as chic as she has been when we were teenagers. No, correction. She is now sleeker and more stylish than ever before. No wonder the designer chose her as one of his catwalk models. He designs exclusively for women over forty. Anais, at any age, is so elegant that she can make the drabbest dress look classy.

I made it to the seat in the front row that Anais had reserved for me. I had attended three faultless rehearsals here during the last two weeks. I was confident that today too would be a huge success. So it was, at least for the first four times that Anais walked down the catwalk. Her neat posture and natural poise displayed the beautiful designs to perfection. Until the fifth time. All was going splendidly. Anais was looking cool, calm and collected in a gorgeous midnight blue creation when suddenly the unthinkable happened. She fell. I jumped up; my hands flew to my mouth. I expected the worst. A twisted ankle. A broken ankle. A broken leg?

She was down right in front of me and our eyes locked. For a moment I saw what I think was a flash of distress, maybe even annoyance. This was quickly followed by a twinkle and a smirk. The smirk promptly blossomed into a glamorous smile as she graciously struggled back onto her heels. She continued confidently down the catwalk, her head held high and her smile unwavering. The crowd stood and cheered.

I could not help but wonder: How on earth did she manage to pull this off and with such unfaltering self-confidence?

Hundreds of thousands of articles and hundreds of books have been written about "How to be a Confident Woman." Should you decide to work with a confidence coach, you will have thousands to choose from on- and off-line. You can subscribe to hundreds of online confidence building courses. There are even apps now that you can download to help you increase your self-confidence.

I wrote this book because I have seen what an increase in confidence can help women achieve. It is my dearest wish that this book will enable women to discover how smart they are and what they can achieve if they are willing to believe in themselves. I did not write this book because I am supremely confident myself or because I know everything about confidence building.

I wrote this book because I hope it will help you become more confident in your abilities as you discover how I deal with my own imperfections and imperfect confidence.

Although I may not be 100% confident myself, I know quite a few women who are. Most of them are French - from there the theme of this book. I thought you might enjoy meeting these women and that you might pick up a few of their confidence secrets along the way. As I have been coaching women for many years, I could not avoid the impulse to add a few "suggestions" of my own to each chapter. I have also included links to useful confidence-building tools that are available on my website, MargarethaMontagu.com. You will find the first of these, a confidence quiz, a bit further down. I hope you find these tools useful.

Finally, I wrote this book because I feel that not enough emphasis is placed what is one of the most important attributes that a confident woman can have: a great sense of humour. I do not think that a woman can be confident if she cannot laugh at herself. Taking oneself too seriously is a great confidence under-miner. I live in a country, and in a specific region of this country, where women excel at not taking themselves too seriously. Women here laugh often and often uninhibitedly. In this part of the world; a good sense of humour is seen as a valuable and absolutely essential commodity.

About the book and what it can do for you

With the help of my five horses, I host personal empowerment work-shops at our house here in the south of France. More than one of our guests has commented on the imperturbable confidence of the local women. They also seem to be under the impression that French women are more confident than women from other nationalities. I am not convinced that this is true. I decided to look into the way French women approach life to see if their approach is different and to see whether this different approach results in them being exceptionally confident. My main aim with this book is to entertain my readers and if a few pearls of wisdom slip into the text, so much the better. The last chapter does give clear guidelines about how to go about adopting the French approach, but it is the only part of the book that is directive. The rest of the book is full of suggestions, but this is not a step-by-step guide of what to do if you want to boost your self-confidence. I believe in "showing," rather than "telling." I think today's women are perfectly aware that there is no one-size-fits-all solution to confidence building. They know that a technique that works for one person may fail miserably for another. This book puts several possible options before you, enabling you to decide for yourself what will work for you and what not.

Each chapter looks at one possible reason why French women may be markedly more confident. I was not born in France, but I have spent part of my childhood here and most of my adulthood. I have a fair amount of experience of the French savoir-faire. In each chapter, I discuss the subject with one of my French friends. I also share some of my own experiences in each chapter. There may also be a few suggestions of how you can incorporate these strategies into your own life, should you choose to do so.

I have created a Playlist on YouTube that you can listen to while you read. It is a collection of French chansons, sung by French chanteuses. Some are older, like Edith Piaf's "Non, je ne regrette rien" and some are more recent like Jennifer's "Tourner ma page." Some are controversial, like Mylene Farmer's "Je te dis tout," some are full of nostalgia like Barbara Patin's "L'Aigle Noir" and some are just about politically correct like Carla Bruni's "Quelqu'un m'a dit."

I wish with all my heart that this book will make a difference to your life.

I hope that you will benefit from it extensively and that it will motivate and equip you to increase your self-confidence dramatically. Mostly, I hope that you will enjoy reading this book and that next time you find yourself in a challenging situation, you may remember how one of my friends solved a similar problem.

Chapter 2

Choosing and Changing your Identity

My understanding of self-confidence is simple. You are a confident person when you know you can handle any challenge that comes your way. You know that you are wise enough, competent enough, experienced enough and clever enough to cope with most situations. Knowing this would imply that you know yourself well. You are intimately acquainted with your strengths as well as your weaknesses. Not all of us are.

Many French women seem to have an unfair advantage in this regard. Many of the confident French women I am privileged to call my friends have a very clear understanding of who they are. Ask any of them. You will immediately, in no uncertain terms, without any hesitation, and with complete confidence be told that they are, first and foremost, 100% French. They are Gascons (from the Gascony region of France). They are from such and such a village where their family has lived for the last five centuries, at least. Go ahead and ask them how they would describe themselves. They will tell you that as French women, they are independent, courageous and highly intelligent. As Gascon women, they are loyal, spontaneous, generous and full of joie de vivre. As a Garreau, Maillard or Ducasse women, they are intelligent, determined and sympathetic. Knowing exactly who you are and what you are capable of can be a great advantage in a stressful situation.

I asked my friend Anaïs, who is serenely confident in all situations, how she manages to be so sure of herself at all times. She explained:

"If I am confident, it is because I know who I am. I grew up in a small village in the Gers. I was brought up by both my parents. Mostly by my mother, as Papa was always busy with the farm. I did not see that much of him. I grew up surrounded by both sets of grandparents, my mother's sister and of her children and my father's brothers and their children. In the same small village, my grandfather's family lived. He had two sisters. Their children and grandchildren lived in our village too.

I had no problem when I was a teenager to figure out who I am. I am Anaïs K, daughter of Jacques and Edith K, granddaughter of Babette and Jean K, sister of Lucas K and cousin of Thierry, Amelie, Marie-Claire and Genevieve.

Our family has lived in the village for many generations, so I was also Anaïs K. from Fenton, a village in the Gers. A Gersois, born and bred and proud of the fact. Gersois people are often convivial, hospitable, passionate, intense and sometimes short-tempered. Knowing this, I also had a good idea of what sort of person I am.

The men and women of my family took part in all the wars that ravaged in this region. We fought in the war against the Black Prince in the 13th century and in all the wars since then, including the Great War. Several members of my family died during the Second World War – both in the front lines and in the service of the Resistance. We are known and respected in the region because of the sacrifices we made. I know I come from courageous, tenacious and strong-willed stock. This helps me when I find myself in challenging situations.

My family has farmed this land for centuries. They were, and are, careful and conscientious farmers. They took good care of the land so that their sons and grandsons would benefit from their investment. We are a family of winemakers. I grew up close to the land. I knew from an early age that there would be a place for me on the farm for the rest of my life.

I am a vigneron's daughter. I learnt the art from my father, my grandfather and my uncles. I also learnt from my mother and my aunts, who looked after the finances and marketing of our wine business. I always loved this way of life, the countryside, the Gers and the people who live here. As you know, my brother is today a lecturer at Pau University, so I took over my father's vineyard. The part of the farm that my father inherited from my grandfather was small. My father managed to buy more land and planted more vines. This means I make a comfortable living doing something I adore and have loved since I was a child. Since most of my family still live in the village, I never have to go far if I need advice about anything! Sometimes we disagree because I want to use newer methods of wine producing. If they give me too much hassle, I just remind them that they used to be called rebel-vignerons in their youth!

Living in a village surrounded my own family meant that I always had friends close by. Several of my cousins were the same age as I was, or a couple of years older or younger. I have heard it said that one's cousins are often the first friends one has in life. That was definitely the case in my life. We were all blessed with the same genes. We had many physical and mental characteristics in common. Many mannerisms too. It not only gave me a sense of who I am but also a sense of belonging. As some of my cousins were older than I was, I always had a choice of role models. Most of my childhood friends also had a clear understanding of who they were and what they were good at. We took this knowledge for granted.

My mother saw early on which way the wind was blowing. She realised that my brother was not interested in taking over the farm. He wanted to study and become an academic. She realised that I was the one who wanted to become a winemaker, so she prepared the way for me. I cannot say that there wasn't any opposition when my father and uncles realised a woman was going to take over my father's estate. I did have a few things going for me: I am a vigneron's daughter. Winemaking is in my blood. I have learnt everything there is to know about winemaking from my father and my uncles. I learnt about the finances and marketing of wine from my mother and aunts. I had the enthusiasm my brother lacked. Eventually, I won the battle. My generation's women have to prove that women can make wine as well as any man. The next generation's women will be accepted as equals, if not better winemakers than men.

You see, the fact that I know exactly who I am makes me confident of my abilities. This knowledge has served me well, making my own way in life and getting to do what I love to do.

I do not know if this type of confidence, based on a clear understanding of one's own identity, is exclusive to Frenchwomen. What I do know is that it has helped several women of my generation convince our own families, and the public at large, that we are as good at making and selling wine as our fathers and forefathers were."

What can you do if you did not grow up with this in-bred knowledge of who you are and where you come from? There is a way you can develop this sort of confidence. You can create your own identity

It has been said that life is less about finding yourself and more about creating or recreating yourself. This makes sense to me. I think that having a strong sense of your own unique identity definitely affects how confident you are.

Defining Your Identity

The rest of this chapter shows you, step-by-step, how to define (or re-define) exactly who you want to be. Having a clear-cut understanding of who you are provides you with a solid foundation to build on. If you lack confidence in yourself, you can start rebuilding your confidence by laying a strong foundation - an unambiguous understanding of who you are.

End of Preview

You can buy Self-Confidence Made Simple as an e-book from various online bookshops including Amazon, Apple, Kobo and Nook.

This book will empower you to
  - make quick decisions in difficult situations based on what is really important to you
  - accept yourself and appreciate your unique talents and abilities
  - believe in yourself so that you can make the changes you want to make in your life
  - deal with stress before it damages your physical or mental health
  - care for yourself physically, mentally and spiritually
  - build strong long-lasting relationships
  - create a solid and reliable support network so that you can
  - ask for help before you feel totally overwhelmed
  - set firm boundaries and say NO without feeling guilty or needing to explain
  - focus on what you can learn from an experience rather on what went wrong
  - realise that whatever age you are at is the best age for you to be
  - stop criticising yourself and
  - celebrate your success without needing to apologise for being brilliant

And much, much more...

Bibliography

- Father William Meninger. Sit down and be quiet. How to practice contemplative meditation November 2013 issue of U.S. Catholic (Vol. 78, No. 11, pages 18-22)
- David S. Black, PhD, MPH1; Gillian A. O'Reilly, BS1; Richard Olmstead, PhD2; et al Mindfulness Meditation and Improvement in Sleep Quality and Daytime Impairment Among Older Adults With Sleep Disturbances: A Randomised Clinical Trial JAMA Intern Med. 2015;175(4):494-501
- Daphne M. Davis, PhD, and Jeffrey A. Hayes, PhD What are the benefits of mindfulness American Psychological Association July/August 2012, Vol 43, No. 7 Print version: page 64
- Kabat-Zinn, J., Lipworth, L., Burncy, R. & Sellers, W. (1986), 'Four- year follow-up of a meditation-based program for the self-regulation of chronic pain: Treatment outcomes and compliance', Clinical Journal of Pain, 2, p. 159;
- Shian-Ling Keng, Moria J. Smoski, Clive J. Robins Effects of mindfulness on psychological health: A review of empirical studies Clinical Psychology Review 31 (2011) 1041–1056
- Baer, R. A., Smith, G. T., Hopkins, J., Kreitemeyer, J. & Toney, L. (2006), 'Using self-report assessment methods to explore facets of mindfulness', Assessment, 13, pp. 27–45.
- Jha, A., et al. (2007), 'Mindfulness training modifies subsystems of attention', Cognitive Affective and Behavioural Neuroscience, 7, pp. 109–19;

- McCracken, L. M. & Yang, S.-Y. (2008), 'A contextual cognitive-behavioural analysis of rehabilitation workers' health and well-being: Influences of acceptance, mindful- ness and values-based action', Rehabilitation Psychology, 53, pp.479–85;
- Ortner, C. N. M., Kilner, S. J. & Zelazo, P. D. (2007), 'Mindfulness meditation and reduced emotional interference on a cognitive task', Motivation and Emotion, 31, pp. 271–83;
- Morone, N. E., Greco, C. M. & Weiner, D. K. (2008), 'Mindfulness meditation for the treatment of chronic low back pain in older adults: A randomised controlled pilot study', Pain, 134(3), pp. 310–19;
- Grant, J. A. & Rainville, P. (2009), 'Pain sensitivity and analgesic effects of mindful states in zenmedi- tators: A cross-sectional study', Psychosomatic Medicine, 71(1), pp. 106–14.
- Brown, Christopher A., Jones, Anthony K. P. 2013, MD, 'Psycho-biological Correlates of Improved Mental Health in Patients With Musculoskeletal Pain After a Mindfulness-based Pain Management Program', Clinical Journal of Pain, 29(3), pp. 233–44.
- Zeidan, F., Martucci, K. T., Kraft, R. A., Gordon, N. S., McHaffie, J. G. & Coghill, R. C. 2011, 'Brain Mechanisms Supporting the Modulation of Pain by Mindfulness Meditation', Journal of Neuro- science, 31(14), p. 5540.
- Gaylord, S. A., Palsson, O. S., Garland, E. L., Faurot, K. R., Coble, R. S., Mann, J. D., et al. (2011), 'Mindfulness training reduces the severity of irritable bowel syndrome in women: results of a randomised controlled trial', American Journal of Gastroenterology, 106, pp. 1678–88.
- Grossman, P., Kappos, L., Gensicke, H., D'souza, M., Mohr, D. C., Penner, I. K., et al. (2010), 'MS quality of life, depression, and fatigue improve after mindfulness training: a randomised trial', Neurology, 75, pp. 1141–9.
- Tang, Y. Y., Ma, Y., Wang, J., Fan, Y., Feng, S., Lu, Q., et al. (2007), 'Short-term meditation training improves attention and

self- regulation', Proceedings of the National Academy of Sciences (US), 104(43), pp. 17152–6.

- C. N. M., Kilner, S. J. & Zelazo, P. D. (2007), 'Mindfulness meditation and reduced emotional interference on a cognitive task', Motivation and Emotion, 31, pp. 271–83;
- Brefczynski-Lewis, J. A., Lutz, A., Schaefer, H. S., Levinson, D. B. & Davidson, R. J. (2007),
- 'Neural correlates of attentional expertise in long-term meditation practitioners', Proceedings of the National Academy of Sciences (US), 104(27), pp. 11483–8.
- Brown, Kirk Warren, Ryan, Richard, M. (2003), 'The benefits of being present: Mindfulness and its role in psychological well-being', Journal of Personality and Social Psychology, 84(4), pp. 822–48;
- Lykins, Emily L. B. & Baer, Ruth A. (2009), 'Psychological Functioning in a Sample of Long-Term Practitioners of Mindfulness Meditation', Journal of Cognitive Psychotherapy, 23(3), pp. 226–41.
- Ivanowski, B. & Malhi, G. S. (2007), 'The psychological and neuro-physiological concomitants of mindfulness forms of meditation', Acta Neuropsychiatrica, 19, pp. 76–91;
- Shapiro, S. L., Oman, D., Thoresen, C. E., Plante, T. G. & Flinders, T. (2008), 'Cultivating mindfulness: effects on well-being', Journal of Clinical Psychology, 64(7), pp. 840–62;
- Lazar, S., Kerr, C., Wasserman, R., Gray, J., Greve, D., Treadway, M., McGarvey, M., Quinn, B., Dusek, J., Benson, J., Rauch, S., Moore, C. & Fischl, B. (2005), 'Meditation experience is associated with increased cortical thickness', NeuroReport, 16, pp 1893–7.
- Davidson, R. J., Kabat-Zinn, J. Schumacher, J., Rosenkranz, M., Muller, D., Santorelli, S.F., Urbanowski, F., Harrington, A., Bonus, K. & Sheridan, J. F. (2003) 'Alterations in brain and immune function produced by mindfulness meditation', Psychosomatic Medicine, 65, pp. 564–70;
- Tang, Y., Ma, Y., Wang, J., Fan, Y., Feg, S., Lu, Q., Yu, Q., Sui, D.,

Rothbart, M., Fan, M. & Posner, M. (2007), 'Short-term meditation-training improves attention and self-regulation', Proceedings of the National Academy of Sciences, 104, pp. 17152–6.

- Epel, Elissa, Daubenmier, Jennifer, Tedlie Moskowitz, Judith, Folkman, Susan & Blackburn, Elizabeth (2009), 'Can Meditation Slow Rate of Cellular Aging? Cognitive Stress, Mindfulness, and Telomeres', Annals of the New York Academy of Sciences, 1172; Longevity, Regeneration, and Optimal Health Integrating Eastern and Western Perspectives, pp. 34–53.

- Eileen Ludersa, Arthur W. Togaa, Natasha Leporea, Christian Gaserb The underlying anatomical correlates of long-term meditation: Larger hippocampal and frontal volumes of grey matter Neuro Image Volume 45, Issue 3, 15 April 2009, Pages 672–678

- Davidson, Richard J. PhD; Kabat Zinn, Jon PhD; Schumacher, Jessica MS; Rosenkranz, Melissa BA; Muller, Daniel MD, PhD; Santorelli, Saki F. EdD; Urbanowski, Ferris MA; Harrington, Anne PhD; Bonus, Katherine MA; Sheridan, John F. PhD Alterations in Brain and Immune Function Produced by Mindfulness Meditation Psychosomatic Medicine: July 2003 - Volume 65 - Issue 4 - p 564–570

- Amishi P. Jha, Jason Krompinger, Michael J. Baime Mindfulness training modifies subsystems of attention Cognitive, Affective, & Behavioural Neuroscience June 2007, Volume 7, Issue 2, pp 109-119

- Fadel Zeidana, Susan K. Johnson, Bruce J. Diamond, Zhanna David, Paula Goolkasian Mindfulness meditation improves cognition: Evidence of brief mental training Consciousness and Cognition Volume 19, Issue 2, June 2010, Pages 597–605

- Sara W. Lazar, Catherine E. Kerr, Rachel H Wasserman, Jeremy R. Gray, Douglas N. Greve, Michael T. Treadway, Metta McGarvey, Brian T. Quinn, Jeffery A. Dusek, Herbert Benson, Scott L. Rauch, Christopher I. Moore and Bruce Fischld. Meditation experience is associated with increased cortical thickness Neuroreport. 2005 Nov 28;16(17): 1893–1897.

- Brown, RP, et al. Sudarshan Kriya yogic breathing in the treatment of stress, anxiety, and depression: part 1-neurophysiologic model. J Altern Complement Med 2005 Apr;11(2):383-4.

- Harvard Medical School. Harvard Health Publications. Stress Management: Approaches for preventing and reducing stress. May 2009.
- Brown, RP, et al. Yoga breathing, meditation, and longevity. Ann N Y Acad Sci 2009 Aug 1172:54-62.
- Seppala, EM, et al. Breathing-based meditation decreases post-traumatic stress disorder symptoms in US military veterans: a randomised controlled longitudinal study. J Trauma Stress. 2014 Aug;27(4):397-405.
- List not exhaustive.